The

ULTIMATE LEADER

The Leadership Style of Jesus

Dr. Gilbert Coleman Jr.

DIVINE HOUSE
B O O K S

No part of this book may be reproduced or transmitted in any form or by any means, electronic or mechanical, including photocopying and recording, or by any information storage retrieval system, except as may be expressly permitted in writing by the publisher. Request for permission should be addressed in writing to Divine House Books - PO Box 682242 Houston Texas, 77268

ISBN: 979-889342722-6

©2024 Printed in the United States of America

BOOK'S OPENING EPIGRAPH

"The authority by which the Christian leader leads is not power but love, not force but example, not coercion but reasoned persuasion. Leaders have power, but power is safe only in the hands of those who humble themselves to serve."
– John Robert Walmsley Stott CBE (April 27, 1921 - July 27, 2011). English Anglican Priest, Evangelist and Theologian. A Principal Author of The Lausanne Covenant 1974. Time Magazine One of The 100 Most Influential People In The World 2005.

BOOK SUMMARY

To meet the ever-changing demands of a world in constant flux, we need leaders who can meet the spiritual, emotional, physical, social, economic and political needs of the people. The sort of leadership that our world is in critical need of was the kind practiced by Jesus Christ. Thankfully, we are not in a dilemma as to how to gain access to His leadership wisdom, as the New Testament exhaustively records His life, teachings and service. His teachings on leadership served as immutable guiding principles for His disciples and present-day leaders in the Body of Christ. In the main, Christ's leadership style was divinely characterized by *compassion, love* and *servanthood*. It is from this triad of attributes that the other virtues effortlessly flow to inspire this remarkable and groundbreaking book on leadership; one in which the author draws richly from the life and ministry of Jesus Christ to propose a model of leadership based on the template of core values that Jesus employed to deliver His message of redemption and deliverance to a world that had tested the forbearance of a loving God to its very elastic limit.

TABLE OF CONTENTS

ACKNOWLEDGEMENTS 1
FOREWORD 3
INTRODUCTION 5

CHAPTER ONE 11
Jesus Had A Vision

CHAPTER TWO 21
Jesus Led With Purpose

CHAPTER THREE 35
Jesus Cultivated A Formidable Intellect

CHAPTER FOUR 45
Jesus Was Focused

CHAPTER FIVE 57
Jesus Led With Love

CHAPTER SIX 73
Jesus Led By Faith

CHAPTER SEVEN 89
Jesus Led With Emotional Intelligence

CHAPTER EIGHT 101
Jesus Led With Courage

CHAPTER NINE 113
Jesus Led With Gratitude

CHAPTER TEN 123
Jesus Was A Servant Leader

CHAPTER ELEVEN 135
Jesus Was A Resilient Leader

CHAPTER TWELVE 147
Jesus Was A Creative Communicator

EPILOGUE 157

ACKNOWLEDGEMENTS

First I must thank my Lord and Savior Jesus Christ for the inspiration to write this book. It is only by His grace that this is happening. Secondly, I am truly thankful for my wife, Debi, of thirty seven years, who continually helps me by providing a loving home environment where I am most comfortable doing my work. Undoubtedly I am most appreciative for Dr Yomi Garnett and his amazing gift that guided me through this literary process. Also Dr Undrai Fizer that I just met recently, who has become an instant friend and now publisher of this book. I also cannot go without thanking the Lord for my Mom and my children that are always a source of great support and encouragement. I love you all without measure!

Gilbert Coleman, Jr.

FOREWORD

The statement that clearly "jumped out at Me," as did others in Gilbert's book, was this: *"A Visionary needs to be connected with other Visionaries. You need to have someone in your life who, like Elizabeth, causes your BABY OF PURPOSE to leap within YOU!"* You need to be involved within intentional life circles; spiritual circles; business circles; creative circles; relational circles; that will provoke, challenge, decree and declare, to the point that Ideas, Strategies, and Solutions, that were once dormant, will be awakened and come alive!

The Leadership of Jesus is just that; a continual relationship with His Divine Spirit of Potential that causes us to rise to our significant capacity of Life. Who we walk with "determines the Capacity of our Becoming!" Who you *are capable of Becoming,* is found within the Mentor and Teacher who challenges you daily.

Our Destiny teaches us within the form of the Holy Spirit. Our Abilities are teaching us within the Energy and Power of the Christ leadership model. Gilbert Coleman (I call him "Gilbert" because he's my covenant brother in The Inter-Global Initiative Leadership Group we founded together) has strategically and creatively "captured the language of leadership" that transcends the common "school of thought" which theorizes "being in charge," and "who's first" in the line. He has captured the essence of the Leader within, being inspired and awakened within the heart, enabling the visionary to ascend to great heights of Spiritual, Mental, and Emotional Exploration of the Kingdom within.

Jesus is the Maker of not only "preachers," but Global Reachers of Humanity. His capacity to "stir the dormant hope" that lies within us, empowering and enabling us to expand to depths we've never known existed, is indeed a "SUPER-POWER" we have been granted access to learn. This Book will help us to grasp not only the language, but the Skill and "Psychological Permission" to Think and Imagine BEYOND THE NORM.

And in this venture, our Leadership Capacity will mature BEYOND THE NORM. It will move into daily experiences and consistent realities of the Super-Natural. We will encounter testimonies of individuals experiencing "the leaping baby" syndrome after having an encounter in your presence. That's it, right? Possessing a Presence which produces Purpose, Destinies, and Dreams? Possessing a Lifestyle which stirs Prophetic Possibilities within many! That's the Christ that Gilbert Coleman is talking about!

I pray that YOU enjoy the "beginning of an incredible journey" into a brand new sphere of Leadership and Lifestyle.

Dr. Undrai F. Fizer, Founder
KAIROS, Inter-Global Inc.

INTRODUCTION

Christ-Centered Leadership

"Let this mind be in you which was also in Christ Jesus, who, being in the form of God, did not consider it robbery to be equal with God." (Philippians 2:5)

To declare that there is a leadership vacuum, not only in this nation, but globally, would be understating a fact that is as despairing as it is tragic. With many so-called leaders perching on a self-centered, egotistical, and manipulative pedestal, and with service to others being as remote from their agenda as the Siberian Desert, it comes as the least bit of surprise that a great number of people are pursuing lives totally void of purpose, potential and destiny since, in any case, they have no credible leaders to look up to, and who can mentor them in the exploration of their own personal gifts and abilities.

Without doubt, history is replete with numerous men and women that have stood out amongst the motley crowd of claimants to the leadership mantle, yet only one man stands head and shoulders above them all. That man is Jesus Christ of Nazareth. There is no doubt that, in His serenity, purity and strength, He embodies all the innate characteristics and abilities that indisputably proclaim one an authentic leader. Equally remarkably noteworthy, Jesus demonstrated these traits with an ease that was both effortless and seamless, since they are and were merely, and in totality, the very essence of His being. Never has there been such a man who served the masses on daily basis, yet never sought recognition, in any form, for all that He did. In fact, His aversion for the awards, citations and proclamations that are the hallmark of leadership in today's world was so total that He insisted that others, be they recipients of His famed benevolence or mere witnesses to His works, remain silent about the great miracles that were credited to Him. The cloak of anonymity that Jesus legendarily craved can only be compared to the nature of water which, feeling no urge to draw undue attention to itself, and although it sustains and nurtures all living things, is perfectly content to discreetly, quietly and effortlessly flow to the lowest spot. That was hardly surprising. Jesus operated from an inner power that rendered it unnecessary to seek applause or fame. Like water, He simply flowed to the lowest spot; that sublime spot where titles and applause do not matter.

At no time in the history of Mankind has it become more compelling than now for each one of us to aspire to the brand of leadership that mirrors the type that Jesus demonstrated. His apostles, at the incipient stage of their tutelage under Him, hadn't an inkling of what lay ahead of them as they willingly opted to abdicate their respective vocations as fishermen and artisans, and follow Him. That decision separated them from the life they had hitherto been accustomed to, and onto one that would irrevocably cast them into a limelight they were ill-prepared for. Each awe-filled day with The Teacher was soaked in mystery and wonder, with humongous crowds clamoring for His presence, even as they hungered for every pearl that fell from His lips. Today's world is lacking in such a teacher-leader that others can gravitate towards. Today's false teacher is so fundamentally flawed in his own knowledge that, rather than be a *fisher of men*, he is pathetically fixated on seeking *"likes"* on Facebook, and *"followers"* on Instagram, while his status as a LinkedIn Influencer is his greatest claim to fame. Tragically, this is the brand of empty leadership; one that is void of the character and substance that credible mentorship demands, that the younger generation are irredeemably doomed to imitate.

Admittedly, the Jesus model undoubtedly sets an extremely high benchmark for leadership. Yet, it provides the only credible template for the individual that may aspire to greatness in his or her lifetime. Even Apostle Paul, in proclaiming that *"Christ is our life!"* also asks us to *"imitate Christ."* The sheer quality of His life and leadership bequeaths us the sort of legacy every human being ought to aspire to. Additionally, the humility of Christ is also inalienably one that the contemporary leader must possess. Men, in particular, seem to naturally possess a certain egotism that lends itself, when it is not kept under leash, to dominance and manipulation of others for personal benefit. Yet, since our best efforts ought to be geared towards making our world a safer and a better place for Mankind, just to be lauded and applauded for the sake of hollow vanity profits us nothing. As Dr Myles Munroe once said, "We should not be seeking followers, but to create more leaders."

Scripture is unambiguous about the fact that we were created to dominate the Earth. Scripture did not prescribe that we dominate each other. Christ-centered leadership does not seek a control of others. Rather, it seeks to teach people to control themselves through genuine self-leadership. Millennials and Gen Z are, without a doubt, some of the most brilliant minds alive today. However, they are also terribly misguided. That is to be expected. Their leaders are, quite often, unbridled and hostile spirits whose only purpose is to seek revenge for the hostilities of the past, as well as the destruction of their own neighborhoods. While we must admit that even Jesus' entourage consisted of some persons of questionable character, they still learned to harness their passions for the purpose of serving mankind. As leaders in the Kingdom of God we are under an obligation to positively impact society with the Christ-centered leadership that will see the kingdoms of this world become the Kingdoms of our God and His Christ.

To meet the ever-changing demands of a world in constant flux, we need leaders who can meet the spiritual, emotional, physical, social, economic and political needs of the people. The sort of leadership that our world is in critical need of was the kind practiced by Jesus Christ. Thankfully, we are not in a dilemma as to how to gain access to His leadership wisdom, as the New Testament exhaustively records His life, teachings and service. His teachings on leadership served as immutable guiding principles for His disciples and present-day leaders in the Body of Christ. In the main, Christ's leadership style was divinely characterized by *compassion, love* and *servanthood*. It is from this triad of attributes that the other virtues effortlessly flow to inspire my humble effort with this book on leadership.

I draw richly from the life and ministry of Jesus Christ to propose a model of leadership based on the template of core values that Jesus employed to deliver His message of redemption and deliverance to a world that had tested the forbearance of a loving God to its very elastic limit. In other words, this book is intended to employ the teachings, life and ministry of Jesus Christ as template for authentic Christian leadership of self and others. The leadership attributes of Jesus Christ are eternally available to us, such that we might *imitate* those same values and virtues to start to walk in the *promise*; walk in the *power*, and walk in the *signs and wonders* of His own miraculous path. It is this compelling need to imitate the leadership virtues of Christ that informs the opening epigraph of the entire book; *"Let this mind be in you which was also in Christ Jesus, who, being in the form* of God, did not consider it robbery to be equal with God." (Philippians 2:5-6 NKJV).

Each chapter of the book is centered around a particular leadership trait that Christ demonstrated during His ministry, and opens with its own epigraph in the form of a scriptural pronouncement by Jesus Christ that eloquently encapsulates the teaching in that chapter. Each chapter concludes with a personal *"Prayer of Focus"* that is designed to elicit *self-examination* and *personal reflection*. Overall, in pointing you directly to Jesus Christ, the ultimate mentor, the book challenges you to evaluate your own leadership style, and to consider time-tested spiritual principles and wisdom that can render you both a more enlightened and a more effective leader.

Happy reading.

Gilbert Coleman

Philadelphia, Pennsylvania

February 2024

CHAPTER ONE
Jesus Had A Vision

"Where there is no vision, the people perish: but he that keepeth the law, happy is he." (Prov 29:18)

The faculty of sight is one of the most important gifts we have from God. Through our eyes, we are able to appreciate the combined *magnificence, splendor* and *beauty* of God's universe. It is also through our sight that the *grandeur* of His creation continues to be made manifest in our lives. I state this with an intentionality that recognizes that we don't necessarily see *with* our eyes. Rather, we see *through* our eyes. In this act of *visual perception,* our eyes act merely as a portal that sends images to the brain where our actual "seeing" is done. What this physiological sequence suggests is that our sight also assists us in our perception of the world around us, and this includes our education, environment, and exposure. It is this perception that determines our responses, and our approach to life.

Being a member of the Body of Christ confers a rather special privilege on us with regards to our perception of the world. In other words, as believers in Christ Jesus, our approach to life is supposed to be vastly different from those who are tragically lacking in a relationship with Him. Life must be lived with *direction*. It must be pursued with *definition*. It must be approached with *discipline*. However, important as these parameters may be, they can never be accomplished in the absence of a clear and unambiguous *reason for living; reason for existing,* or *reason for being,* a notion the French elegantly express with the quaint phrase, *raison d'être.* This all-important reason is what we term *purpose*, and it is an engine that runs on a vehicle called *vision.*

You will need a vision. That is because the starting point of a life lived in purpose will always be a vision. Vision is the vehicle on which the entire engine of purpose runs. What you see with your *inner eye* is indicative of your power as a visionary. Ordinary people see physical beauty. Extraordinary persons; members of the Body of Christ, see the divine attributes that are a reflection of God's magnificent splendor. Such people are also those who understand that their primary reason for being privileged to be here on Earth is to be co-creators with God as the inheritors of His kingdom here on Earth. The vision of a believer is borne of the *spiritual chariot* of creative imagination. That vision is the emotive force that drives everything else in a believer's life. Vision is the ability to see beyond current reality. Vision is the innovative competence to invent that which is not yet in existence. Vision is a believer's acumen to transform, in the present moment, into the future form.

Vision, more than any other factor, will affect the choices a believer makes. Naturally, that is why vision also dictates, to a significant degree, how time is deployed, and what energy is deployed to. That is why, more often than not, persons of vision constantly remind themselves that it hardly matters what they are doing if what they are doing is not what matters most. To be a visionary is, for all practical purposes, to be a dreamer. Convinced of the possibilities and potentials of your dreams, you are more than likely to refuse to back down, or be discouraged by the challenges that will inevitably be thrown on your path. Instead of throwing in the towel,

CHAPTER ONE: Jesus Had A Vision

you will find a way to sustain the positive and unrelenting attitude that allows you to continue to drive positive change in your life. A vision will give you the enduring capacity for converting obstacles into the tools that will end up working in your favor.

Purpose is undeniably linked to vision. The dawn of each new day ought to infuse a certain exhilaration and exuberance into our being as we anticipate those events of the day that will ultimately bring the manifestation of what the Lord has placed within us, and which will make life tremendously better for ourselves and for others. It is almost inconceivable that there is anyone on Earth whose wish is to endure a meaningless existence. To live each day without a connection to the day before it, and a certain hope for the day after it, is to live a hollow life void of impact. The apostle Paul made a very dangerous statement in his First Letter to the Corinthians, *"Imitate me, just as I also imitate Christ." (1 Corinthians 11:1-6).* We must admit that statement borders on the supercilious as he solicits an inspection of his life for flaws. Yet, perhaps it is only that sort of arrogance that he felt could sufficiently arrest the attention of his seriousness to the seriousness of his teaching. He invites us to observe his daily walk as one we all should aspire to. I would wager that very few in Christendom today would dare make such a seemingly immodest statement. That is because the inconsistencies in our Christian walk are all too glaring, being almost invariably a total and despairing departure from the life that the Lord Jesus lived while He was here on Earth.

Let us turn our attention to focus on His life, one that was exemplary in being the embodiment of all that the Father had envisaged for mankind at creation. He was a man who demonstrated exactly who we were intended to be, had the events at the beginning of creation not conspired to thwart that intention. It often boggles my imagination at how Adam and Eve, though having been exposed to God, would instead opt to hearken to any other voice but His, and allow those fateful moments of misguided decision-making truncate their beautiful destiny, and irrevocably alter the course of human history. In the same instance, we must swiftly turn our attention to a beautiful shrub that dwelt in the presence of God for eternity, yet knowingly rebelled against Him, while also leading insurrection in glory. This is the tragic saga of Mankind.

Scripture records that Jesus came to Earth as the full embodiment of humanity, while remaining in the fullness of God. *"For in Him dwells all the fullness of the Godhead bodily." (Col 2: 9).* We are also placed in no doubt whatsoever that, from a very tender age, He was in full awareness of His mission on Earth. At the age of twelve years, a disturbing encounter took place between Jesus and his "earthly parents." They had attended the festival in Jerusalem as usual. After the celebration was over, they started home to Nazareth, unaware that Jesus had stayed behind in Jerusalem. His parents didn't miss him at first. Later, they had to go back to Jerusalem in search of him, and finally found him in the Temple, sitting among the religious teachers, listening to them and asking questions. *"His mother said to Him, "Son, why have You done this to us? Look, Your father and I have sought You anxiously." And He said to them, "Why did you seek Me? Did you not know that I must be about My Father's business?" (Luke 2:48-49).*

Clearly, Jesus began to engage in independent thought from that early age, and one can only surmise that He was listening to a voice that was totally distinct from a worldly one. When, like Jesus, we become inextricably linked to our vision, our perspective, and our approach to life will undergo a drastic transformation. We must understand that Jesus was by no means being disrespectful to His parents. In any case, Joseph and Mary had already been forewarned that the child in their custody was not of this world. In today's world, we approach scripture with a Western eye. Our American approach to scripture often prevents us from seeing matters as they really are. We must attempt a different perspective if we are to attain proper comprehension. That is why early attainment of vision places us on a different trajectory altogether from others and will, quite often, be unacceptable to those closest to us. *"Then the multitude came together again, so that they could not so much as eat bread. But when His own people heard about this, they went out to lay hold of Him, for they said, He is out of His mind!" (Mk 3: 20-21).* As I stated earlier, one's vision provides discipline for the journey. The lack of understanding, and the opinion of others, should never distract us from our divine mission. There was never a time when Jesus was internally conflicted as to what He should be doing at any given time. Therefore, each one of use, without hesitance, should be willing to champion His example. *"For to this you were called, because Christ also suffered for us, leaving us an example, that you should follow His steps." (1 Pet 2: 21).* Life is not a divine experiment, but a project of providence to fulfill a purpose that your generation is in dire need of. The example of Jesus would become a statement to His generation, and to generations yet to come. That is why our life cannot, and should not be lived in isolation. Admittedly, our journey will inevitably be attended by moments of isolation, but such moments are merely supposed to serve us as course correctors.

Every generation has challenges it must address, and God, in His infinite wisdom, assigns such problems to those He has accorded the necessary tools and gifts to address them. The frustration for so many is that they labor under the burden of discovering exactly what problem the Lord has sent them to Earth to solve. In keenly observing the landscape of our society and culture, it is easy to see that many have arrived at their wits end as to what to do with their life, a quest than often leads along the erroneous path of committing some sort of sinister act against humanity. What is worse is that the heinous crimes are committed without thought of the repercussions and consequences incident to such egregious felonies. These tendencies are perfectly validated in scripture. *"Do not be deceived: Evil company corrupts good habits!" (1 Cor 15: 33).* I like to think in terms of how Elizabeth was stimulated by the presence of Mary. The Bible says that Elizabeth's baby, John, leaped in her womb, and she was filled with the Holy Spirit.

A visionary needs to be connected to other visionaries. You need to have someone in your life who, like Elizabeth, causes your *baby of purpose* to leap within you; someone who ignites the flame of passion and ingenuity within you. As we continue to peruse the life of Jesus, it becomes very clear and evident that He had that effect on every town He set foot in. *"But Jesus withdrew with His disciples to the sea. And a great multitude from Galilee followed Him, and from Judea and Jerusalem and Idumea and beyond the Jordan; and those from Tyre and Sidon, a great multitude, when they heard how many things He was doing, came to Him." (Mk 3: 7-8).* Vision is an embodiment of tremendous foresight. It confers the ability to see what is happening in the present, while providing a portal to foresee and foretell the future. The generality tend to think that people who live life through the lens of their vision are living in a fantasy world. The response of the disciples when Jesus talked about going back to Jerusalem after being threatened with death is a case in point. He was responding to the request of Mary and Martha, Lazarus' sisters, who sent word that Lazarus was sick. Jesus said, *"....Our friend Lazarus sleeps, but I go that I may wake him up." (Jn 11:11).* But He also said that Lazarus' sickness was not unto death, but for the glory of God and His Son to be revealed. For someone who is not Kingdom-minded, these are difficult statements to digest.

Another dimension to vision is that it also provides *definition*.

CHAPTER ONE: Jesus Had A Vision

Clarity is essential when following the plan of God. Each time Jesus went away to pray, He would come back to delineate the agenda for that day to the disciples. In fact, He didn't even select the disciples until He had been in prayer all night long. *"Now it came to pass in those days that He went out to the mountain to pray, and continued all night in prayer to God. And when it was day, He called His disciples to Himself; and from them He chose twelve whom He also named apostles." (Lk 6: 12-13).*

Vision also possesses *timing*. Not only did Jesus know *where* He was supposed to be, but He also knew *when* He was supposed to be there. Just because a matter is urgent to someone else does not necessarily make it important to you. I will discuss the matter of relative *urgency* and *importance* at length in another chapter. We easily recall that Jesus was not moved by the fervent emotional appeal in Martha's request for her brother, Lazarus. When we are following the dictates of vision, the feelings and emotions of others cannot become the indicators of what we are supposed to respond to. *"Now Jesus loved Martha and her sister and Lazarus. So, when He heard that he was sick, He stayed two more days in the place where He was. Then after this He said to the disciples; Let us go to Judea again." (Jn 11: 5-7).* The disciples could not believe their ears. They were stymied by His statement, as they were secure in their belief that His return to Judea would spell danger, and very possibly imminent death. Even contemporary thought suggests a seeming callousness and coldness in Jesus not departing swiftly to go and attend to someone He claimed He loved. Yet, we need to understand that Jewish culture at that time held that anyone that had been dead for four days was certainly *dead*, and any notion of resurrection was totally out of the question. Therefore, Jesus' arrival was merely in keeping with the culture, while all the more assuring that only God got the glory when Lazarus was raised from the dead.

It must be fully understood that Jesus was capable of anything as the *Son of God,* yet chose to impose limitations on Himself as the *Son of Man* for, if that were not the case, no mortal would be able to relate to Him. Additionally, He stated that we would be capable of doing *"greater works"* than Him, a suggestion that seemed totally far fetched considering the magnitude and multitude of the miracles He performed. What is equally astonishing is that He accomplished all those feats in just three and a half years. Clarity about one's vision will always assist a person in doing things that far exceed what the average person might be able to accomplish, a feat that eludes the average person because of a lack of focus on what and why they were sent to Earth. Jesus doesn't just give us a standard. He *is* the standard. True leaders should always be desirous of ensuring that those that they lead ultimately become better than them. The best player on a team is not great until fellow team members are greater still. Jesus had no reservations whatsoever about releasing the disciples to do the work that He Himself was doing. *"Then He called His twelve disciples together and gave them power and authority over all demons, and to cure diseases. He sent them to preach the Kingdom of God and to heal the sick." (Lk 9: 1-2).* Even though Jesus Himself was limited in time and space, He still had a vision for a world that would ultimately reflect the Kingdom of heaven. Unfortunately, many in the modern day church do not share that vision. We have become so immersed in fulfilling our own agenda that we have all but jettisoned the Biblical mandate to fill the whole Earth with the knowledge of His glory. The vision of any ministry should be to help all believers become mature sons and daughters of God that will continue to spread love and hope to a lost and dying world. This has nothing to do with aspiring to celebrity status. I have come to observe that we spend more time celebrating and evangelizing ourselves than the communities and neighborhoods that we have been sent to minister to. Elaborate buildings and flashy presentations may have an attractive veneer to them, but that was not the presentation Jesus offered.

Elaborate edifices, such as cathedrals, have replaced the core essence of visionary ministry as exemplified by Jesus. A cathedral, by its pre-eminent status as the principal church building that accommodates the episcopal presence of a Bishop, is almost always a grand structure, usually constructed with such scrupulous attention to architectural detail that its magnificence and splendor is nothing short of a glorious and splendid monument to the awesome might of God. *That may well be all true.* Yet, authentic glorification of God rests, not on the gigantic pillars, marble floors, richly-upholstered vestries, expansive aisles, and stately pulpit of the cathedral. The real structure of the church will have to find a resting place in the fabric of love that ought to be woven into the totality of the existence of the cathedral as a place of worship of an awesome God. *It is, however, a matter of sad commentary that, while God asks that His church be built with pillars of love and the fabric of kindness, men bring stones to build cathedrals.* Jesus never craved notice or attention. He craved such a degree of anonymity that He might as well have been hiding from Himself! He was like water. He flowed to the lowest spot. in fact, after performing a miracle, He would advise the people to say nothing about it. *"Let this mind be in you which was also in Christ Jesus, who, being in the form of God, did not consider it robbery to be equal with God, but made Himself of no reputation, taking the form of a bondservant, and coming in the likeness of men." (Phil 2: 5-7).* The conclusion is clear. To even remotely aspire to a vision of greatness, we must first cultivate a vision of humility.

Prayer of Focus

"Lord, accord me vision to recognize that I am privileged to be here on Earth to be an inheritor of Your kingdom here on

Earth. Give me wisdom to convert vision to the most potent motive for my actions. Give me grace to deploy my time, and my energy, to my vision, for it hardly matters what I am doing, if what I am doing is not what matters most. Accord me discipline to strategically pause to ask myself what the most valuable use of my time is in this moment, such that every moment of my Earthly existence is devoted to enduring vision for the actualization of my Earthly assignment. In Jesus Name. Amen."

CHAPTER TWO

Jesus Led With Purpose

"The function of leadership is to produce more leaders, not more followers." - Ralph Nader

Without singular exception, Jesus Christ included in that dispensation, each and everyone of us is *deployed* to planet Earth to fulfill God's divine plan. I use the term *deployed* with conscious and deliberate intent. Although the word *deploy*, like any other, seeks application in many different forms of expression, it achieves more common usage in military parlance, with the word itself implying the movement of troops and arsenal into strategic position for military action. By a similar token, God has deployed us as His troops, so that we can strategically position ourselves for the *purposeful* dominance of the Earth He created for the expression of our purpose. That is why it equates to a sad state of affairs to live a lifetime in blissful ignorance, if not in total unawareness, as to why you exist in the first place. That the search and the discovery of life purpose is an individual quest is not in dispute. In any case, no one can lead another person to a destination that they are not familiar with. At some point, each one of us must ask him or herself the question, *"Why on Earth am I on Earth?"*

For the generality, each day is merely a monotonous repetition of what is, at best, a humdrum existence, and at worst, a despairing and vicious cycle of boring and unproductive regularity. The Lord'scommand to the first man and woman to occupy Earthly space was to be fruitful, and to multiply. On the surface, that statement seemingly and simply lends itself to the need to procreate to populate the Earth. Yet, the statement has more context to it than mere procreation, for which, in any case, He who created the Earth most probably already had a foolproof blueprint. The context of the statement accommodates the wider notion of being limitlessly productive, and to abundantly flourish, in all the faculties that the Lord blessed us with. We must exert all effort to ensure that we do not waste time and energy doing the wrong thing. No enterprise could possibly be worse than climbing a tall ladder, only to arrive at the top and discover that your ladder was, all the time, leaning against the wrong building. It is also akin to courting the lamentable disaster of climbing a mountain only to arrive at its peak and discover that you have climbed the wrong one.

To lead with purpose is to acknowledge that situations will not always be at their most ideal for leading with ease, and to accept that fact as a mere part of the territory of leadership, and adjust accordingly. That is why true leaders are those who are capable of courageously confronting challenges, often of the most daunting sort. In the course of His ministry, Jesus was often confronted with such extraordinary circumstances, yet remained undaunted in His mission. Not only was He compelled to endure the hypocrisy of the religious leaders of the day, He also had to patiently deal with the unbelief of the people He encountered from one town to the next. When one, in addition, considers the heavy-handed manner with which the Roman government of the day administered justice and governance, one is presented with the picture of a situation in which to minister the word of God becomes nothing but a Herculean task. *"For it is not possible that the blood of*

CHAPTER TWO: Jesus Led With Purpose

bulls and goats could take away sins. Therefore, when He came into the world, He said: "Sacrifice and offering You did not desire, But a body You have prepared for Me." (Heb 10: 4-5).

There is a fundamental purpose to leadership. It is to replicate leadership for an uninterrupted continuum. In other words, in being, in all essence, a *train-the-trainer* enterprise, it is to produce leaders, and not to produce and maintain a retinue of followers. To a point of unerring exactitude, Jesus knew the length of the tenure of His ministry on Earth. Therefore, it became a matter of the most imperative for Him to adequately groom and prepare the apostles to succeed Him in His extraordinary ministry, and ultimately carry on the work without Him. It is noteworthy that, at different times, He advised them of the imminence of His departure, and by what manner He would leave, but for some reason or the other, they were never quite capable of grasping His message. *"Then He commanded His disciples that they should tell no one that He was Jesus the Christ. From that time Jesus began to show to His disciples that He must go to Jerusalem, and suffer many things from the elders and chief priests and scribes, and be killed, and be raised the third day. Then Peter took Him aside and began to rebuke Him, saying, "Far be it from You, Lord; this shall not happen to You!" But He turned and said to Peter, "Get behind Me, Satan! You are an offense to Me, for you are not mindful of the things of God, but the things of men." (Mt 16: 21-23).*

Right from the outset, it behoves us to understand that the Father is not impressed by our hard work and persistence. He is only interested in the sense of purpose we deploy to our assignment. All that Jesus did in the course of His Earthly ministry was borne of divine purpose. The fundamental utility of purpose is that it serves as the guiding Northern Star that tells us not only when to show up, but also how to show up. That means we ought to be consistently driven by a spirit of excellence, where the words *average* and *mediocre* become unacceptable. When we are purpose-driven, we will also be decisively-driven. Most certainly, no one desires to follow someone who is perennially vacillating between ideas and concepts, in the process never really accomplishing anything worthy of note. *"Now the Passover, a feast of the Jews, was near. Then Jesus lifted up His eyes, and seeing a great multitude coming toward Him, He said to Philip, "Where shall we buy bread, that these may eat?" But this He said to test him, for He Himself knew what He would do." (Jn 6: 4-6).* Jesus already knew what to do! He knew what to do because He knew His *purpose* to an unerring point of clarity. A leader with *purpose* knows what to do because he knows his *purpose*.

But, what does it mean to lead with purpose? To simplify matters, and to avoid confusing intellectual jargon, I will draw from the leadership example of Moses to illustrate what it means to lead with purpose. Although he grew up in the palace of the Egyptian Pharaoh, Moses never lost sight of his Hebrew heritage. When Moses saw an Egyptian beating a Hebrew slave, *"..... he looked this way and that way, and when he saw no one, he killed the Egyptian and hid him in the sand." (Exodus 2:12).* It wasn't a crime that could be long hidden. Pharaoh found out what Moses had done, and tried to kill him. Moses ran for his life. Later, God chose Moses to rescue the Israelites from Egypt. Moses was afraid, and he gave one excuse after the other, one of which was that he stuttered. To overcome that fear, God recruited his brother, Aaron, to assist him. Moses rose to the challenge. Through the story of the ten plagues and Pharaoh's opposition, he finally led the Israelites out of Egypt. When they were trapped between Pharaoh, who suddenly changed his mind to pursue slaves he had only newly freed, and the Red Sea, Moses told the people, *"...... Do not be afraid. Stand still, and see the salvation of the LORD, which He will accomplish for you today. For the Egyptians whom you see today, you shall see again no more forever. The LORD will fight for you, and you shall hold your peace." (Exodus 14:13)*. Moses was right. By the power of God, he led them through the Red Sea on dry ground. That was just the beginning of Moses' *courageous* and *purposeful* leadership.

The job God called Moses to do was fraught with difficulties and challenges. Moses never hid his emotions from God. They spent forty days together on top of Mount Sinai, where God gave Moses the two tablets of the covenant law. Meanwhile, the people became tired of waiting for Moses. They made an idol, and started worshiping it. This made God angry. He offered to kill all the Israelites, and make Moses into a great nation instead. "Then Moses pleaded with the Lord his God, and said: *"Lord, why does Your wrath burn hot against Your people whom You have brought out of the land of Egypt with great power and with a mighty hand?" (Exodus 32:11)*. God listened to Moses, and He did not act on His emotions. For forty years, Moses led the Israelites, and God kept His promise to always be with him, even when Moses allowed his anger to get the better of him, which disallowed him from entering the promised land.

Moses abandoned a privileged life to pursue his true life purpose. He grew up in the imperial palace of the wealthiest, and certainly the most advanced civilization in that part of the world. He probably received what might have easily been the equivalent of today's Ivy League education. Yet, he abandoned all that privileged station in life to pursue the loftier purpose of identifying with his own roots and people. Although Moses trusted God in the midst of some of the most difficult circumstances imaginable, he remained an ordinary and flawed mortal. But then, God does not ask us to do things that we can accomplish on our own. He calls us to do things that are impossible without Him. *Ultimately, God does not call the qualified, He qualifies the called for purposeful leadership.*

One's life purpose should never be viewed as a burden, but as a passion. In fact, in the context of this discussion, the words *purpose* and *passion* almost assume a curious sort of interchangeability, with passion being the inalienable driver of purpose. You can no more express your life purpose without passion, any more than you can deploy passion to anything other than purpose. You were placed on this Earthly plane to magnificently manifest the precise purpose that renders you a living testimony to the phenomenal genius that is the Divine. Tragically, you fail to manifest that *purpose* because you have all but abandoned any attempt at earning the authentic life that is truly a life of *passion*. That passion continues to lie dormant within you until you decide to unearth the purpose that perfectly complements it.

Purpose provides us with both *insight* and *foresight.* As I stated earlier, purpose dictates when we should show up, and how we should show up. No one single individual is assigned to everything, and to everyone, no matter how seemly talented or skilled on multiple fronts. That is why scripture eloquently refers to our work as *"Body Ministry."* Permit me to explain. Based on New Testament teachings regarding the Body of Christ, John Robert Stevens, Founder of The Living Word Fellowship of the 1950s, defined the term "Body Ministry" as the ministering of believers, one to another, that is both directed by, and exalting of, Jesus Christ. Stevens wrote that he anticipated, *"A layman's church where every member has a ministry, a rewarding function in the church, and a rich walk in the Lord."* He described the Body of Christ as an interdependent reality, where each person is valued and needed by God, and by each other. Rather than relying on one leader to minister to every person, the members of the Body of Christ are supposed build one another up in love. *"...but, speaking the truth in love, may grow up in all things into Him who is the head; Christ, from whom the whole body, joined and knit together by what every joint supplies, according to the effective working by which every part does its share, causes growth of the body for the edifying of itself in love."* (Eph 4:15-16). The synopsis of Stevens' theory is that we have moved away from the *one-man ministry*, which is no more than a *one-man show*, and onto the *Body Ministry*, the emphasis being no longer on the individual, but on the corporate ministry. The concept of Body Ministry de-emphasizes the role of the leader as the only one God has appointed to minister His word. Rather, ministry should now be seen as a great glorification of the Lord, moving through many human vessels. Let us not be under any illusion as to our human limitations. Physical fatigue and mental exhaustion will become the plight of the man or woman who spends the majority of their time attempting to tie up all the loose ends. *The loose ends will never end.* We have a good example in our Lord. At no time do we see Jesus in a frenzy because He was unaware of what He ought to be doing at any given moment. Therefore, it must be understood that leadership does not begin with people, but with an individual that has defined their purpose.

Adam and Eve were given a divine mandate of purpose at creation, but were too naive to fully embrace that charge. Let us devote some thought to it. They were supernaturally-empowered beings with no life experience whatsoever. Let us fast forward human evolution, and juxtapose their situation with today's man and woman. Today, the generality have the life experience, but could care less if their life has any significance or meaning. Purpose seeks to express itself in transformation for the overall good. It is no wonder, then, that today's world languishes in abject despair because the majority have never become truly acquainted with their life purpose. Yet, a life lived with purpose is a life lived with *meaning*. That means purpose is what gives meaning to our existence by offering us a sense of direction, helping to guide us in alignment with our goals and objectives. That is why the discovery of life purpose is, for all practical purposes, synonymous with the discovery of the real meaning for one's existence. When Jesus proposed to Peter and the other disciples to follow Him, He was not looking for followers, but men that He could transform into leaders. *"And Jesus, walking by the Sea of Galilee, saw two brothers, Simon called Peter, and Andrew his brother, casting a net into the sea; for they were fishermen. Then He said to them, "Follow Me, and I will make you fishers of men." They immediately left their nets and followed Him." (Matt 4:18-20).*

Therefore, we can draw the conclusion that true leadership begins with self-discovery. We were created to lead, and designed to dominate. Jesus was never confused about His identity. *"The Pharisees therefore said to Him, You bear witness of Yourself; Your witness is not true. Jesus answered and said to them; Even if I bear witness of Myself, My witness is true, for I know where I came from and where I am going; but you do not know where I come from and where I am going." (Jn 8: 13-14).* Cultural orientation has all but prevented many of us from becoming the leaders we were created to be. We are afflicted with the same tragic lack of self-confidence that Gideon and Moses used to convince themselves of their lack of competence and capacity to carry out their divinely-ordained tasks. Yet, both men went on to accomplish some of the greatest deeds of early Old Testament history. We easily recall that their initial response to the Lord was that He must have chosen the wrong person!

One of the greatest failings of our times is that our educational system does not teach students to become employers. It programs them to become employees, the net result of which is a preponderance of followers, and a paucity of leaders. In the educational system, tests and examinations are even termed "standardized." Worse, I have found that, in many ways, people are actually penalized for being outstanding.

CHAPTER TWO: Jesus Led With Purpose

Without doubt, not a few of us would have been told, *"You're too high minded!"* or *"That is simply impossible!"* Such statements invariably sound the death knell to the dreams and aspirations of those who do not possess mastery of their own thoughts. *Sadly, no one fact about human nature is more baffling that the fact that the generality tend to place a higher premium on the opinion of others about them than their own opinion of themselves.* Dominion is not an impartation. It is the combined result and effect of our comprehension of the mysteries and principles of the Kingdom. People in the secular world, no matter how brilliant and cerebral they may be, tend to think entirely differently from Kingdom citizens. *"They are of the world. Therefore they speak as of the world, and the world hears them. We are of God. He who knows God hears us; he who is not of God does not hear us. By this we know the spirit of truth and the spirit of error."* (1 Jn 4: 5-6). That fruit that awaits ripening in our life will be based on our ability to understand the systems of the Kingdom.

Expressed differently, there are certain dimensions of access to matters of the Kingdom we will never experience if we do not possess the proper understanding and insight. *"And I will give you the keys of the kingdom of heaven, and whatever you bind on earth will be bound in heaven, and whatever you loose on earth will be loosed in heaven."* (Mt 16: 19). The ultimate motivation for human activity must always remain celestial and human good, and not necessarily human desire, which, in itself, is motivated purely by vanity and selfish ego. In order to render ourselves amenable to the leadership model of Jesus, we must be selfless, and not selfish. Incredulous as it may sound to the ordinary ear, Jesus never had a thought that was totally original to Him. I know that sounds almost implausible, but nonetheless remains as true as His gospel. *"I can of Myself do nothing. As I hear, I judge; and My judgment is righteous, because I do not seek My own will but the will of the Father who sent Me."* (Jn 5:

30). What this translates to in mortal reality is that we can possess all the potential in this world, but if we are lacking in vision, all of our efforts will be met with futility. *That is because, vision is the ability to see as it should be, not as it is.* The key to effective leadershipis unflinching belief in the potential of one's creative skills and resources to accomplish one's objectives. Yet, there is another aspect to that equation. That belief must be coupled with near-absurd confidence in one's abilities. The beautiful utility of our confidence is that it disallows the spirit of doubt to permeate our thinking. In the final analysis, dear brethren, leadership is 80% attitude and 20% skill, and that is why those who are skilled, perhaps even uncommonly so, tend to end up working for those who come to vocational equity with the right attitude.

I once heard someone say, *"Show me a man for whom the word impossible does not exist, and I'll show you a man unto whom all things are possible."* It is true. Jesus consistently demonstrated that there was no such thing as *impossible*. *"When Jesus heard it, He departed from there by boat to a deserted place by Himself. But when the multitudes heard it, they followed Him on foot from the cities. And when Jesus went out He saw a great multitude; and He was moved with compassion for them, and healed their sick. When it was evening, His disciples came to Him, saying, "This is a deserted place, and the hour is already late. Send the multitudes away, that they may go into the villages and buy themselves food." But Jesus said to them, "They do not need to go away. You give them something to eat. And they said to Him, "We have here only five loaves and two fish." He said, "Bring them here to Me." (Mt 14: 13-18)*.

Purposeful leadership does not acknowledge the *minimum*. Rather, purposeful leadership exploits all ways to use the *minimum* to achieve the *maximum*. I hasten to add that, while in no way does this suggest that we lose touch with reality, we remain under an inalienable obligation to disallow that

CHAPTER TWO: Jesus Led With Purpose

which appears to be impossible to dampen our faith. Think of those times when Jesus was not even remotely close to the person to be healed, and all He did was speak words of faith that brought healing to an individual located at a place of considerable distance from Him. In today's world, people are in dire need of leadership that will provide more than baseless hope. What people need are leaders who will be undaunted in their ability to lead others into fertile places of growth and maturity. A true leader's vision becomes the platform or standard for their own life, and also becomes the impetus to be a solo artist, should that become compellingly necessary. *"Then Jesus said to them, Most assuredly I say to you, unless you eat the flesh of the Son of Man and drink His blood, you have no life in you. Whoever eats my flesh and drinks My blood has eternal life, and I will raise him up at the last day. For My flesh is food indeed and My blood is drink indeed. 60) Therefore many of His disciples, when they heard this, said, this is a hard saying; who can understand it (66-67) From that time many of His disciples went back and walked with Him no more. Then Jesus said to the twelve; Do you also want to go away? (Jn 6: 53-55; 60; 66-67).*

The Master's message was clear, unambiguous and unequivocal. *You are free to leave at any time!* In no way was their departure going to prevent the actualization of His vision, and the fulfillment of His mission. The prime lesson here is that the vision given to us is not *incumbent* upon who goes or who stays, but on the visionary's commitment, no matter the circumstances. There are people who actually labor under the totally misguided illusion that your vision will completely fall apart at the seams if they deprive you of their involvement in it. Nothing could be further from a truth that also recognizes that no one; simply no one, should be so indispensable that they are accorded that sort of leverage. The disciples often demonstrated their ineptitude as soon as Jesus was not with them to provide direction and discipline for the task at hand. At such times, their fear was always as palpable as the palpitations of their hearts, and were it not for the calm and stolid assurance of the Master might quite easily have abandoned their assignment.

A purposeful leader breathes and breeds a certain confidence that cannot be shaken, whatever the magnitude of what lies before them. They understand that those working alongside them can easily wilt under pressure if they are not shown that fear is not only needless, but unnecessary. *"Now I know that the Lord saves His anointed; He will answer him from His holy heaven with the saving strength of His right hand. Some trust in chariots, and some in horses; but we will remember the name of the Lord our God."* (Ps 20: 6-7). It is at such times that Jesus' perception takes center stage. Scripture presents us with many settings in which He was acutely aware of the thoughts of the people surrounding Him, and He never shied away from bringing those thoughts into question. This suggests that, for a purposeful leader to know how to appropriately respond to all situations, and at all times, he or she must remain in acute awareness of his or her environment. In the same breath, this also calls for a critically honest assessment of our stance on any matter, to gauge what our proper response should be, and to determine whether the current scenario is in the best interest of the led.

True leaders think clearly and lucidly, because of which they know what to look for, and what to be on the lookout for. The true leader's decision is made in accordance with unalloyed purpose. As I stated earlier, purpose provides the discipline that disallows one from making hasty, impulsive, and irrational decisions. Scripture does not share with us one moment in which Jesus veered from His divine purpose. Even though His was an Earthly assignment, it definitely had a heavenly purpose to it. It was, and is, a far cry from the Father's divine intention to see Earth become a microcosm of heaven. The tragedy of this age is that contemporary culture has become inundated with the despairing sense of entitlement and bloated egotism that stand as hindrance to the wholesome furtherance of the gospel, and the expansion of the Kingdom of God. The allure of the past seductively blinds the people to the information that is designed to bring them into alignment with who they were originally created to be. To make matters infinitely worse, present day leadership is trapped in the twisted and perverted thinking that is merely self-serving for them and for their acolytes. Suffice it to conclude that this manner of leadership only prevails because of decades of the existence of a lawless and Godless society that wants little or nothing to do with anything that remotely suggests a God-fearing lifestyle. Nonetheless, no matter what the mindset of the people might have have been, Jesus never allowed it to deter Him from His heavenly assignment and purpose. What is more, no matter what the mindset of the people of this generation may be, the commission of Christ will remain sacrosanct and inviolable until He returns to validate the establishment of His Kingdom of purpose on Earth.

Prayer of Focus

Lord, as I stand before You today, I humbly ask for clarity of purpose. Help me understand the unique path You have laid out for me. Guide my steps and illuminate my heart, so I may walk confidently in the direction You have intended for me. As I navigate the choices before me, grant me the gift of discernment. Open my eyes to recognize the paths that align with Your will and those that lead astray. Help me make decisions that honor You and contribute to my purpose. With discernment, I can confidently follow the path You have set, avoiding distractions and detours. Thank You for guiding me toward alignment with Your divine plan. In Jesus Name. Amen.

CHAPTER THREE

Jesus Cultivated A Formidable Intellect

"The heart of the prudent acquires knowledge, And the ear of the wise seeks knowledge." (Prov 18:15)

The *Merriam-Webster* dictionary defines intellect as *"the power of knowing, as distinguished from the power to feel and to will."* It also defines intellect as *"both the capacity for knowledge, and the capacity for rational or intelligent thought, especially when highly developed."* In the study of the human mind, intellect is the ability of the human mind to reach correct conclusions about what is *true*, and what is *false* in reality, and how to deploy the thinking faculty to solve problems. The word *intellect* derives from the Latin word, *intelligere*, ("to understand"), from which the term *intelligence* in the French and English languages is also derived. Intellect is often used to describe *intensive reasoning* and *deep thinking,* particularly in relation to subjects that spark deep discourse, such as literature or philosophy. The word *intellectual* is a noun that describes a cerebral person who engages in deep thinking, as evident in historical figures like Aristotle, Shakespeare and Albert Einstein. Jesus was a man of superior intellect. He was a man of sharp and superlative intellect. That should hardly come as a surprise for, on the spiritual pedestal, intellect is the *executive assistant* of wisdom, and it can do right only when it faithfully carries out the instructions of its principal, *wisdom*.

We often fail to appreciate that the human essence of Jesus or, if you will, His humanity, co-exists in prefect tandem with His deity. He was very much a man as He was very much God. The implication for Him was that He had to acquire knowledge, and to experience life, as a man while He was here on Earth. It is because no one can live on Earth without occupying a *body* that, had Jesus not presented Himself to us in *bodily* form, we simply would have been helplessly unable to relate to Him at any level of interaction, and we would have simply dismissed Him as an illegitimate entity, human or divine. This brings us to Adam. Adam failed because he fell into disobedience. We must forgive him. The truth is that, even though he was made perfect, he suffered the fatal inadequacy of not passing through a process of maturation. In other words, Adam was created a full grown man. We are now in a salutary position to draw a sharp contrast between Jesus and Adam. Jesus was birthed as a child, and was compelled to pass through the process that all other human beings go through. As both a theologian and a minister, I have had cause to wonder about how useful for our fuller understanding it might have been if we had been exposed to information about His matriculation into manhood. The best snippet of information the Bible offers us in that regard was what His life was like at the age of twelve.

In those days, it was customary for the Jews to travel to Jerusalem to celebrate the annual Feast of the Passover. In the year of Jesus' twelfth birthday, His parents traveled to Jerusalem in accordance with that custom, at the conclusion of which they set out for the return trip. Unknown to them, the Boy Jesus had lingered behind in Jerusalem. That was the era in which people traveled in caravans, explaining why Jesus was not initially missed as they made their way back home. It was assumed that He very possibly was with other family members somewhere in the caravan. On that assumption, they had gone a whole day's journey before they realized He was not among their relatives and acquaintances. They returned to Jerusalem, looking for Him. Scripture reveals that it took them three days to finally locate Him, and when they did, He was in the temple sharing and receiving knowledge from the Rabbis. *"Now so it was that after three days they found Him in the temple, sitting in the midst of the teachers, both listening to them and asking them questions. And all who heard Him were astonished at His understanding and answers." (Lk 2:46-47).* His parents were understandably amazed. *"His mother said to Him, "Son, why have You done this to us? Look, Your father and I have sought You anxiously." And He said to them, "Why did you seek Me? Did you not know that I must be about My Father's business?" But they did not understand the statement which He spoke to them." (Lk 2:48-50).*

What is eminently curious about this narrative, however, is that at no time did Joseph and Mary seem to recall the foreknowledge they had been accorded by an angel that the child they were rearing was no normal child. We must appreciate that Jesus' matter-of-fact reply to His parents is to be in no way misconstrued as insolence and disrespect. Being very clear about *who He was, what He was sent to do,* and *when He was supposed to do it,* He was merely being unambiguously true to Himself, and to others, His parents inclusive. It boggles the mind, even that of a minister of the Word like myself, to even make a remote attempt at imagining what it must have been like for Him, being human while at the same time possessing the mind of God! What is altogether astounding is that He was at all times able to rein in His divinity, such that He could function exclusively as a human while here on Earth. *"Then He went down with them and came to Nazareth, and was subject to them, but*

His mother kept all these things in her heart. And Jesus increased in wisdom and stature, and in favor with God and men. (Lk 2: 51-52).

As a leader, Jesus possessed a formidable intellect, one that manifested itself quite early in His life, and in no uncertain terms, going by His precocious discussion with the astonished scholars and teachers of Jewish law and doctrine. In any case, it strains imagination to even conceive that Jesus could be Lord if He were not of sound intellect. Could divinity ever be remotely synonymous with stupidity? Let's face it, Christian perspective of Jesus in all other respects would be rendered invalid if He weren't the best informed and most intelligent person of all time. Expressed succinctly, Jesus will simply have to be the most intelligent person who ever lived, bringing us the best information on the most important subjects. Lest we forget, John's gospel, in the words, *"In the beginning was the Word, and the Word was with God, and the Word was God,"* commences its narrative by identifying Jesus as the *Logos,* which is theologically defined as the Word of God, or principle of divine reason and creative order, identified in the Gospel of John with the second person of the Trinity incarnate in Jesus Christ. That means, by implication, *Logos* is not merely a word but an intelligent, rational thought. *Logos* is the root of our word *logic,* and Jesus as the *Logos* is the embodiment of *logic.* He used logic and logical reasoning throughout His ministry. His aim in utilizing logic was not to win battles, but to elicit understanding or insight in His audience. We see many instances of this display of intellectual sparring in His ministry. We see it in how he challenged the woman of Samaria at the well.

"Will you give me a drink?"

"How is it that you, a Jew, ask a drink of me, a woman of Samaria?"

Chapter Three: Jesus Cultivated A Formidable Intellect

"If you knew the gift of God, and who it is that is saying to you, 'Give me a drink,' you would have asked Him, and He would have given you living water."

"Sir, you have no bucket, and the well is deep."

"Everyone who drinks of this water will be thirsty again, but those who drink of the water that I will give them will never be thirsty. The water that I will give will become in them a spring of water gushing up to eternal life."

"Where can one get this living water? Are you greater than our father, Jacob, who gave us this well, and drank from it himself, as did also his sons and his livestock?"

"Everyone who drinks this water will be thirsty again. But, whoever drinks the water I give them will never thirst. Indeed, the water I give them will become in them a spring of water welling up to eternal life."

"Sir, give me some of your own water, so that I will never become thirsty again, and have to keep coming here to draw water."

"Go back home, and come back here with your husband. I am waiting."

"I have no husband."

"You are right when you say you have no husband. The fact is that you have had five husbands, and the man currently in your life is not your husband. What you have just said is quite true."

"Sir, I can see that you are a prophet. Our ancestors worshiped on this mountain, but you Jews claim that the place where we must worship is in Jerusalem."

"Woman, believe me, a time is coming when you will worship the Father, neither on this mountain nor in Jerusalem. The

problem with you Samaritans is that you blindly worship what you do not know. We worship what we do know, for salvation is from the Jews. Yet a time is coming; in fact it has already come, when the true worshipers will worship the Father in the Spirit and in Truth, for they are the kind of worshipers the Father seeks. God is spirit, and his worshipers must worship in the Spirit and in Truth."

"Sir, I know that He who is called The Messiah, also called Christ, is coming. When He comes, He will explain everything to us."

"I, the one speaking to you; I am He."

Only divine intellect could have conducted this dialogue at such a sublime level. The church today needs to start to acknowledge this aspect of Jesus' nature. The irony is that, while we lament that our institutions of higher learning have kicked God out of the classroom, the church appears bent on kicking the professor out of the pew. I will explain. To what degree is the church infusing sufficiently vigorous intellectual message into sermons, such that a professor can look forward to attending church, and see his attendance as both a time of spiritual revival and intellectual stimulation? As a leader, Jesus did not water down the intellectual content of His messages. He tasked the intellect of His audience, in much the same way He tasked the intellect of the Samaritan woman. We must stop watering down our messages, so that we can continue to stretch the intellect of our congregations to make them spiritually and mentally intelligent.

The Bible is silent on the life of Jesus from the time He was twelve years of age until His emergence into full scale ministry at the age of thirty. We are left with no option than to imagine that He attended school at the synagogue with the other children. Again, we are best advised to remember that, although He learned the ways of the world just as we did, His approach to the issues of life was entirely different from ours for the simple reason that He had none of man's sinful blood in Him. I find myself envious of Jesus for living a life totally free of sin, even though He was presented with all of the same temptations that each us face on a daily basis. *"For we do not have a High Priest who cannot sympathize with our weaknesses, but was in all points tempted as we are, yet without sin." (Heb 4: 15)*. Scripture makes it clear that His thinking came from a superior Source. Because of the presence of the Holy Spirit in our life, we possess the same power and capability. Our constraint, however, is that we have become totally immersed in the ways of the world, making them a hindrance, and a road block to the discovery of the leader that lives inside of each of us. We have developed a *follow the leader* mentality that hinders us from being the *original* leader we were created to be. Yet, what was quite evident about Jesus was that He did not suffer any awkwardness from being different from everyone else. He was secure in His own skin. What is it about us that compels us to lean more toward *assimilation* than toward *distinction?* Yet, only *originals* will make their mark in the world, and not *copies!*

Remarkably, even though Jesus possessed a brilliant mind, He yet remained teachable. He demonstrated to us that no matter how old one may be, or the degrees one may have acquired, we must remain amenable to instruction. This holds true, most especially for those privileged to be in leadership positions. Just because we hold leadership positions does not make us infallible repositories of knowledge. In my opinion, the day we stop learning is the day we start dying. *"Though He was a Son, yet He learned obedience by the things He suffered. And having been perfected, He became the author of eternal salvation to all who obey Him." (Heb 5: 8-9)*. No matter the encounter, Jesus was never lacking in the proper response to what He was confronted with. The religious leaders of the day would, time and again, try to trap

Him with His own rather weighty words, but their attempts always ended up an abysmal exercise in futility. *"Then they came again to Jerusalem. And as He was walking in the temple, the chief priests, the scribes, and the elders came to Him. And they said to Him, by what authority are You doing these things? And who gave You this authority to do these things? But Jesus answered and said to them: I also will ask you one question, then answer Me, and I will tell you by what authority I do these things; The baptism of John, was it from heaven or from men? Answer Me! And they reasoned among themselves, saying, if we say, from heaven, He will say, why then did you not believe him? But if we say, from men, they feared the people, for all counted John to have been a prophet indeed. So they answered and said to Jesus, we do not know. And Jesus answered and said to them; Neither will I tell you by what authority I do these things."* (Mk 11: 27-33).

There is a certain brilliance that each one of us can possess if we are willing to divest ourselves of years of errant teaching that for the most part has steered us away from the wisdom that is divine. Jesus cautioned the disciples on numerous occasions not to allow themselves to be deceived by information that came from contaminated sources. *"Now when His disciples had come to the other side, they had forgotten to take bread. Then Jesus said to them: Take heed and beware of the leaven of the Pharisees and the Sadducees. And they reasoned among themselves, saying, it is because we have taken no bread. But Jesus being aware of it, said to them; O you of little faith, why do you reason among yourselves because you have brought no bread? Do you not yet understand. Or remember the five loaves of the five thousand and how many baskets you took top? Nor the seven loaves of the four thousand and how many large baskets you took up? How is it you do not understand that I did not speak to you concerning bread? But to beware of the leaven of the*

Pharisees and Sadducees. Then they understood that He did not tell then to beware of the leaven of the bread, but of the doctrine of the Pharisees and Sadducees." (Mt 16: 5-10).

No matter how anointed we may be, intellect remains a necessity, which is why I often suggest to leaders to read other books apart from the Bible. There is no way we can adequately address the ills of our society and culture without understanding the thinking of our generation. At creation, when Adam and Eve were confronted by the serpent, scripture characterizes him as the most "subtle" (clever) beast of the field. That is why we are obligated, if only for the reason of self-preservation, not to take our enemy lightly, and the only way we can succeed at that is by becoming well versed in the thinking of our world and its people. Jesus Himself made a very profound statement about the mentality of the world's people. *"So the master commended the unjust steward because he had dealt shrewdly. For the sons of this world are more shrewd in their generation than the sons of light." (Lk 16: 8).* This statement is a clear indictment of the children of God. The life of Jesus should be a challenge to us all to, not only go to church to listen to eloquent and soul-inspiring messages, but to also grow in the *spiritual intellect* that is the combined *grace* and *knowledge* of our Lord and Savior, Jesus Christ. Each one of us should always desire to expand our mental capacity. Christ was brilliant beyond his chronological years and the people recognized it. *"Now about the middle of the feast Jesus went up into the temple and taught. And the Jews marveled, saying, How does this Man know letters, having never studied. Jesus answered them and said; My doctrine is not Mine, but His who sent Me." (Jn 7: 14-16).* In the final analysis, there is absolutely no way you can become a man or woman of intellect if you do not take study as an imperative. The word study does not imply mindless consumption of ineffectual literary material, but the reading of wholesome and uplifting literature that can complement the eternal wisdom contained in scripture. We must remain ever mindful of Paul's challenge to his spiritual son, Timothy, *"Study to show yourself approved unto God, a workman (skilled craftsman) who does not need to be ashamed, rightly dividing the word of truth." (2 Tim 2: 15).*

Prayer of Focus

Lord, beam your Light of Grace upon my intellect, and dissipate the darkness of sin, and of ignorance that covers me. Grant me a penetrating mind to understand. Accord me a retentive memory. Bless me with method and ease in learning. Give me the ability to grasp knowledge, and the abundant grace to express myself with incomparable lucidity. Guide my work, direct its progress, and bring it to successful completion. In Jesus Name. Amen.

CHAPTER FOUR

Jesus Was Focused

"And when He had sent the multitudes away, He went up on the mountain by Himself to pray. Now when evening came, He was alone there." (Mt 14: 23).

Today's world offers, not only a plethora of temptations that appear maliciously designed to distract us from our divine destiny, but also the desire to attempt to access all that appear to be for our own good without going through God to get it. While, fortunately, there are many who are able to escape these traps of human frailty, there are far too many who don't. Yet, the rather tragic reason for this dilemma is that the generality are in total ignorance of the reason for their occupation of earthly space in the first place, and are therefore incapable of connecting with that which can render them productive of a life that is both fulfilling and abundant. The crucial question then becomes, *"What sets you apart from the billions of inhabitants of Earth?"*

Once you are able to lock into what you were created to do on Earth, you will start to develop a certain *self-confidence,* and it is that confidence that will establish first, a *direction* for your life, and then a *focus* on that direction, and finally the *discipline* to sustain that focus. What self-confidence does for you is to boost that innate sense of self-belief that renders you certain of imminent success, and it is that certitude that, in turn, will motivate you to do all in your power to actualize that success. What this translates to is that a certain price, known as *sacrifice*, is demanded of the person desirous of attaining any degree of success in life. *"Enter by the narrow gate; for wide is the gate and broad is the way that leads to destruction, and there are many who go in by it. Because narrow is the gate and difficult is the way which leads to life, and there are few who find it." (Mt 7: 13-14).* For instance, if you lack the requisite skills, you will acquire them. If you are deficient in knowledge, you will acquire it. If matters turn out not quite as anticipated, you will creatively find a solution to rectify the situation. What your self-confidence does is to set you up for the success that subsequently reinforces your self-worth, leading you to even more and greater success. Even though your starting point may have been the same as others, your self-confidence alone is sufficient to take you much further than someone who doesn't have it. Self-confidence is one of the greatest assets you could possibly possess. Not only does it make you feel better emotionally and mentally, but it also unconsciously propels you toward achieving your goals. Self-confidence gives you the belief that you can conquer your challenges, no matter how insurmountable they may seem. Expressed simply, self-confidence is a prerequisite for focusing on your goals. In fact, we can safely declare that lack of confidence, in itself, is a monumental distraction. Because Jesus had confidence in Himself, He was able to focus on His mission with confidence. He knew He could, and would not fail.

Most dictionaries allude to a definition of focus as the ability to concentrate and sustain one's attention. Interestingly, when it comes becoming distracted from our *issues of focus*, we appear to be at far greater risk from the *tug and pull* of others than from our own whims and caprices. Indeed, it is this external *tug and pull* from those who seem to believe

CHAPTER FOUR: Jesus Was Focused

that they know what is best for us that we must adamantly resist, and vehemently guard against. Almost invariably, such people will be relentless in their attempts to persuade us to follow their instructions, or make ourselves amenable to their suggestions. Let us make no mistake about the truth that, in our affairs, no human voice should ever be louder than God's voice. The enemy of our soul would love nothing better than to see us fail. The enemy is not particularly bothered about your past or your present, and it is only when we take meaningful steps toward our future that he becomes upset with us. If the stark truth be told, the greater majority of us simply have not learnt the power inherent in one of the smallest words in the English language; *no!*

No one could distract Jesus. As a leader, His laser beam focus was such that He could not be swayed from His mission by eloquent words, nor could He be deterred from vital tasks by the most passionate of emotions. Without doubt, His total fixation on His purpose led to some tense moments when those around Him, including even His family, felt that He was *losing His mind,* all because His approach was perceivably anything but conventional. *"Then the multitude came together again, so that they could not as much as eat bread. But when His own people heard about this, they went out to lay hold of Him, for they said He is out of His mind!" (Mk 3: 20-21).* It is not difficult to imagine how challenging matters might be if and when we *go against the grain* of public opinion. In fact, such pressure could be so unbearable and unrelenting that we might easily buckle under it. Despite all the ridicule, Jesus remained focused on the task at hand.

Jesus subscribed to the emphatic *no!* As enticing as some of the suggestions and invitations that came His way were, when Jesus said *no!* that was exactly what He meant. *The Lord always says what He means, and He always means what He says.* To fulfill destiny, we must learn to tread the, quite often, excruciatingly lonely path. More often than not, others will misconstrue your confidence for arrogance, if not outright superciliousness. Yet, to stay focused almost always entails deciding whether we are going to please God, or please Man. Jesus was committed to pleasing Him who sent Him. *"After these things Jesus walked in Galilee; for He did not want to walk in Judea, because the Jews sought to kill Him. Now the Jews Feast of Tabernacles was at hand. His brothers therefore said to Him; Depart from here and go into Judea, that Your disciples may also see the works that You are doing. For no one does anything in secret while he himself seeks to be known openly. If You do these things, show Yourself to the world. For even His brothers did not believe in Him. Then Jesus said to them: My time has not yet come, but your time is always ready. The world cannot hate you, but it hates Me because I testify of it that its works are evil. You go up to this feast. I am not yet going up to this feast, for My time has not yet fully come. When He said these things to them, He remained in Galilee." (Jn 7: 1-9).*

People are perfectly ready to offer us as much distraction as we are misguidedly willing to accept. One of the powerful secrets to focused living is simply to remain steadfast in the faithful pursuit of one's life purpose. Refuse to be distracted by life's minor offerings. The truth is that many, being only too aware of your short attention span, will approach you with crumbs from the *table of life*. Their intention is really quite simple. It is merely to steer you away from a course for which they both envy and resent you. Flee from such individuals. No matter how many fruits you pluck from our Lord's *tree of life*, it will not dry up. It will simply keep producing more *fruit*, in the form of a productive life worthy of Him. Our Lord's *tree of life* is particularly legendary for its tenacity of fruitfulness, which also translates to its tenacity of purpose. Remain as productive, and as committed, as the *tree of life* that is perennially fruitful, and not as impotent as the *tree of Man* that dries up just because one person has plucked fruits from it. For many, life is no more than a rollercoaster of fun-filled experiences at the amusement park of life. Quite frankly, there is more than sufficient entertainment to fill that void in us that continually seeks amusement. Yet, there surely must be more to life. I propose that there must be more to life than just spending our time appeasing our flesh, as opposed to seeking the fulfillment of what we have been given to do that will ultimately effect sustainable and radical change in our society, and our culture. We must all do everything in our power to de-emphasize the cheap thrill in our life.

One is aware that many would consider Jesus a poor example of exemplariness in anything, for the simple reason of His divine nature. Yet, as I took the pains to laboriously point out in the previous chapter, we would do well to always remember that all of His actions, and His activities, while He was here on Earth, were carried out purely in His capacity as a man. It is not for absolute nothing that, in more than a hundred instances in the gospels, He was referred to as the Son of Man. It is my firm conviction that Jesus' ability to remain so focused on His mission had infinitely more to do with His prayer life than anything else. Indeed, a great number of the miracles He performed came only after He had spent the entire night in prayer. If the unalloyed truth be told, the post-modern contemporary church receives a dismal failing grade when it comes to concentrated and committed prayer. *"And when He had sent the multitudes away, He went up on the mountain by Himself to pray. Now when evening came, He was alone there." (Mt 14: 23).* This passage eloquently suggests that if we are going to receive explicit instructions from our heavenly Father, we must submit to times of solitude in prayer. It is very difficult to hear properly when we are surrounded by those who are not truly fixated on purpose.

Apparently, one particular *night* of prayer was singularly important to Jesus. *"In these days he went out to the* mountain to pray, and all night he continued in prayer to God." (Lk 6:12). How totally extraordinary! It appears that Jesus was praying for wisdom to know whom to select as his twelve apostles. This is a perfectly reasonable conclusion since the first thing Jesus did after praying is to choose His twelve apostles. Not only that, at least going by Matthew's account, before settling on His apostles, Jesus exhorted the disciples to pray. What is more, He told them to pray thus, *"The harvest is plentiful, but the laborers are few; therefore pray earnestly to the Lord of the harvest to send out laborers into his harvest."* (Matt 9:37). Jesus told his disciples to pray for workers. It is also reasonable to assume that Jesus was praying for workers, too; specifically the workers who would be his apostles.

The pertinent question is: *Why did Jesus, the totally focused Son of Man, pray?* Again, the answer is to be found in the fact that Jesus is both *God* and *Man*. As the eternal Son of God, Jesus prayed out of His divinity, serving as a display of communion with His Father. Being one with the Father, there is no reason to be surprised that the Son communicated with the Father. In that sense, Jesus' prayer life is rooted in His divinity. Yet, Jesus prayed out of His *humanity* as well, serving as a model for us of what dependence on the Father ought to look like. Clearly, Jesus lived a dual life of *trust in* and *dependence on* His Father to lead Him, including leading Him to the twelve men preordained by God to represent Jesus on earth. Regardless of why Jesus prayed, there is much to learn from Him.

Jesus' prayer life teaches us that *prayer is necessary.* We should never be too busy to pray. We often fall back on so many platitudes for not finding the time to pray. We have to sleep, after all. We have to work, after all. We have to take care of the kids, after all. When all those things we have to do are done, there is hardly any time left for prayer, meaningful or otherwise. At least, that is what we tell ourselves. Yet,

CHAPTER FOUR: Jesus Was Focused

the sacrosanct truth is that we need prayer as surely as we need sleep, food and rest. Each of us relies on God, and we demonstrate this reliance by praying. Jesus had the weight of the world on His shoulders, yet He prayed. *Prayer demands solitude.* It is noteworthy that Jesus got away from the crowd in order to pray. He sought a place of quiet. Although there is no specific scriptural command for us to pray in solitude, we are obliged to take to heart the model of our Lord. We should make it a personal discipline to unplug from the world before we speak to the Creator of that world. I recall the story of a woman who ran an orphanage. She literally had no place of escape from all *her children.* She found solitude in the corner of the kitchen, with her apron pulled over her head to allow her just a few moments to think and pray.

Prayer will often demand strenuous effort. On that mountainside Jesus continued to pray all night. He once rebuked his disciples for failing to stay awake and pray. *"Then He came and found them sleeping, and said to Peter, "Simon, are you sleeping? Could you not watch one hour?" (Mk 14:37).* Because He is fully *man,* Jesus felt the need to sleep and rest. Yet, He believed it was more important for Him to stay alert and pray. Nothing should make us think our prayer life should be easy. Persistence ought to be the hallmark of every believer's prayer life. We are to plead with God *faithfully, fervently,* and *passionately. Prayer must be purposeful.* Jesus had *real* work to do. His apostles must be chosen. These apostles would go on to preach and write the words the Spirit would use to build the church. Jesus had a church to establish, and so He prayed. When we pray, we ought to know what needs to be accomplished.

Jesus teaches us that *prayer is effective.* Having stayed up all night talking to His heavenly Father, Jesus was ready to pick twelve men to serve Him on earth. Jesus prayed, the Father answered, and Jesus chose the twelve. Jesus prayed because he knew no decision is outside the will of the Lord.

But having prayed, Jesus acted. He stepped out and selected the men He believed were best suited to do the work He needed done. Likewise, we pray, because we know that God is sovereign. Then, we act, trusting that God will guide our steps. *"............The effective, fervent prayer of a righteous man avails much. Elijah was a man with a nature like ours, and he prayed earnestly that it would not rain; and it did not rain on the land for three years and six months. And he prayed again, and the heaven gave rain, and the earth produced its fruit." (Ja 5:16-18).*

Jesus is an exemplary model for us in prayer. Yet, we must be careful not to see Jesus only as our example in prayer. This is because if we see Jesus merely as a prayer example, seeing how spectacularly well He prayed may be so demoralizing for some of us, believing we have fallen too short of the mark. Though we must hold Jesus as a model to follow, if He is only a model, we will surely fail. In other words, although prayer is a discipline we must improve upon, we must also appreciate the fact that the path to better prayer is not fundamentally praying because Jesus prayed, but praying because Jesus died and rose again. It is through this death and resurrection that we find more than an example, and we find a Savior who bore the wrath of God that we deserved, took the debt of sin that we accrued, and declared us righteous. That is grace, and having received such plentiful grace, we pray, not merely because Jesus prayed, but because Jesus died to give us hearts that long to pray.

Think of focus in this manner. You are trying to watch one of your favorite programs on TV, but there is someone else in the room that is bent on holding a conversation that you have the least bit of interest in. It is both a distraction and an irritating intrusion, and you wish they would be quiet. Being focused on our God-given assignment must be viewed in much the same light. If we are going to be focused as Jesus was, we have to be single-minded. This means that

CHAPTER FOUR: Jesus Was Focused

we have to prioritize our relationship with God above all else. In many ways, some of us have intense relationships with other people that seem to supersede our relationship with the Father. Yet, He has said that He will not tolerate us placing anyone else before Him. *"If anyone comes to Me and does not hate his father and mother; wife and children, brothers and sisters, yes, and his own life also, he cannot be My disciple." (Lk 14: 26).*

I hasten to say that He is not telling us to literally hate them, but to make sure that they never come before Him. An element of the modern day Christian life is that we are more inclined toward a life of *inspiration* rather *transformation*. The apostle Paul shared with us that we are to be transformed by the renewing of our mind. *"And do not be conformed to this world, but be transformed by the renewing of your mind, that you may prove what is that good and acceptable and perfect will of God." (Rom 12: 2).* At the moment of salvation we are supposed to be desirous of the *"newness of life,"* such that old things begin to pass away, and all things should become new. I will be the first to admit that this is a challenging proposition, but it is not an insurmountable challenge if you want Him, and not just the things that He gives. In the Kingdom of God, straddling the fence is unacceptable. We cannot have one foot in the Kingdom and the other in the world. *It is all or none!*

Scripture demonstrates an inherent trait in Jesus that was His perseverance in the face of any and all difficulty, or adversity. Some believers have been deceived into thinking that once we accept Christ, all of our problems are over. The truth is that in many ways, our troubles are just beginning. Let us bear in mind that after being baptized and anointed by God, Jesus did not immediately enter into ministry, He was tested. *"When all the people were baptized, it came to pass that Jesus also was baptized; and while He prayed, the heaven was opened. And the Holy Spirit descended in bodily form like a dove upon Him, and a voice came from heaven which said, "You are My beloved Son; in You I am well pleased." (Lk 3:21-22). "Then Jesus, being filled with the Holy Spirit, returned from the Jordan and was led by the Spirit into the wilderness, being tempted for forty days by the devil. And in those days He ate nothing, and afterward, when they had ended, He was hungry. (Lk 4: 1-2).*

We can see that hunger did not deter the Master from totally focusing on the assignment before Him. At some point, we all have to ask ourselves one question, *"What is really most important?"* The focus and emphasis should be on eternal values as opposed to temporary ones. Nothing about Earth is permanent. The Bible is quite clear that heaven and earth are going to pass away. *"While we do not look at the things which are seen, but at the things which are not seen. For the things which are seen are temporary, but the things which are not seen are eternal." (2 Cor 4: 18).*

Jesus was never swayed from the fact that He was given an earthly assignment with a heavenly purpose. Our responsibility is to know that we are not here to advance the church, but to advance and expand the Kingdom of God.

The enemy of our soul has used social media to devise a very clever trap to entice us. All we desire are the "likes" and "followers" on social media, as opposed to seeing souls come into the Kingdom. *"The fruit of the righteous is a tree of life, and he who wins souls is wise." (Prov 11: 30).* We are also fixated on the "proper branding." What this suggests is that we are more concerned about presentation than power. *"Go your way; behold, I send you out as lambs among wolves. Carry neither money bag, knapsack, nor sandals; and greet no one along the road." (Lk 10: 3-4).* Indeed, we are called not to crave fanfare, but to just do the work. There should be nothing that this world has on offer that has such an allure that we are distracted from our relationship with God.

Prayer of Focus

Lord, allow me to stay on purpose by re-directing my focus. Give me that plan of action that will allow me to 'stay on purpose,' and to follow through with what I set out to accomplish. Allow me to focus on that which I want, as long as it is in accordance with Your Will. Allow me to focus on where I want to go, as long as it is Your determined destination for me. The power to do what needs to be done comes from knowing my purpose, and as long as I remain on that purpose,' my 'why' will be so strong that my 'how' will find itself falling effortlessly into place. In Jesus name. Amen.

CHAPTER FIVE
Jesus Led With Love

"Love is patient, love is kind. It does not envy, it does not boast, it is not proud. It does not dishonor others, it is not self-seeking, it is not easily angered, it keeps no record of wrongs. Love does not delight in evil but rejoices with the truth. It always protects, always trusts, always hopes, always perseveres." (1 Cor. 13:4-7).

The moment Adam and Eve fell in the Garden of Eden appears to have spelled doom for the overall quality of Man as a beloved creation of God. Not only does the moral fiber of mankind continue to witness a daily assault on all fronts, but even the very fundamental and primordial thread of love that is supposed to bind us together as children of God is getting more and more tenuous with each passing day, even as we are no longer even merely inching, but rather taking leaps and bounds away from each other, thanks to an individual narcissism and a collective cynicism. We have deviated from God's original plan for us. We are at a place that is a far cry from what the Lord desired for us, and from us. In Rom. 8:35, the apostle Paul asks a rhetorical question, *"Who shall separate us from the love of Christ? shall tribulation, or distress, or persecution, or famine, or nakedness, or peril, or sword?"* Viewed from a very fundamental context that might not even demand the exertion of effort in theological analysis, the answer to that question is simply that it is Man himself that has separated himself from the love of Christ.

Let us approach matters from first principles. God's love for His creation has always been very evident. For instance, He did not place Man on Earth until every provision for his sustenance had not only been created, but provided in lavish abundance. More Instructively, however, through His divine foreknowledge, He knew only too well that mankind was going to disobey Him and, to provide for the mitigation of even this misdemeanor, a very benevolent God had already instituted the plan for our salvation and redemption. *"Blessed be the God and Father of our Lord Jesus Christ, who has blessed us with every spiritual blessing in the heavenly places in Christ, just as He chose us in Him before the foundation of the world, that we should be holy and without blame before Him in love. (Eph 1: 3-4).*

The love of God, which is our birthright, is unique. Today's world is dismally lacking in that sort of love. It is extremely difficult to even imagine the existence of that sort of love. The Bible states very clearly that the Lord loves us with an everlasting love. In literal terms, this means His love for us is inexhaustible. However, the Bible also shows us how, from one generation to the next, His people have spurned the Lord's love, even unto this present day. The Old Testament is replete with stories of how, time and again, Almighty God attempted to demonstrate His love by delivering His chosen people from what could have been complete annihilation, but His love was met with indifference, sometimes to such a degree of belligerence that they made a decision that they no longer wanted Jehovah to lead them, and would rather have a king like all of the other idolatrous nations. Let us fast forward to the present day. Our culture is infamously garnished with barely-concealed insolence toward God and, rather, love for our fellow man, which often comes at a

CHAPTER FIVE: Jesus Led With Love

prohibitive premium.

Jesus was the physical embodiment of the love of God. Whereas many of us would pick and choose who we will embrace, as opposed to having and sharing love with all of mankind, Jesus loved everyone. More often than not, He was found in the company of people who, according to the prevailing culture, He ought never to associate with. The religious order of the day made it a point to accuse Him of the supposedly gross misdemeanor of daring to be seen with men or women that were considered "sinners." *"Now it happened, as Jesus sat at the table in the house, that behold, many tax collectors and sinners came and sat down with Him and His disciples. And when the Pharisees saw it, they said to His disciples; Why does your Teacher sit with tax collectors and sinners? When Jesus heard that, He said to them, Those who are well have no need of a physician, but those who are sick." (Mt 9: 10-12).*

If the unbiased truth be told, sometimes it appears that it is so much easier to notice the love people have for you than the love God has for you. The reason for this is really quite simple. You can physically witness the presence of these people, and the way they express their love. There is a stark difference with the experience of God, making it truly challenging to understand the extent to which He loves you. After all, none of us can physically see Him on this side of Heaven. That is why God gave us His Word. His Word is designed to help us understand who He is, and how much He really does love us. Throughout the Bible, God is described as an all-powerful and eternally-just God. But, He is also described as being deeply loving to those He created. In the entire biblical saga, God is presented as a character who strongly cares for us, so much so that He even allowed His Son, Jesus Christ, to enter this world to orchestrate a restored relationship with humanity. In fact, Jesus is the physical embodiment of God's eternal love, showing us that His love is a real and tangible entity that we can cling to, and put our hope in, rather than just an abstract concept we can't even begin to understand. Let us dwell for a moment on the very pertinent, and very accurate, meaning of biblical love.

"Love is patient, love is kind. It does not envy, it does not boast, it is not proud. It does not dishonor others, it is not self-seeking, it is not easily angered, it keeps no record of wrongs. Love does not delight in evil but rejoices with the truth. It always protects, always trusts, always hopes, always perseveres." (1 Cor. 13:4-7). There are many different kinds of love. There is parental love. There is brotherly love. There is romantic love. At the mention of the word *love*, we often first associate it with anything from dating to sex. Yet, the word is so much broader than we often realize. According to the above passage, *biblical love is simply putting the needs of others before ours.* All of us fall short of the expectation set by this passage at some point. This is because selflessness does not come naturally to us. *"For all have sinned and fall short of the glory of God." (Romans 3:23).* The good news of the Gospel, however, is that God perfectly embodies the four verses in I Corinthians 13: 4-7. He created love in the first place. In turn, this means that God is *love* itself. *"He who does not love does not know God, for God is love." (1 John 4:8).* And because He is love, He displays this quality not only through His words, but through His actions as well. *"As a father has compassion on his children, so the Lord has compassion on those who fear him." (Psa. 103:23).* As any good father would, God feels sentimental about His children, and shows affection toward them. This picture of God as the perfect Father is a deeply intimate one because it illustrates how far He would go to keep us safe and secure. Another illustration of God's love is seen in Hosea 2:14-23. Rather than a father this time, this Bible passage describes a faithful husband that comforts and treasures his wife. This is also meant to be a metaphor for God's devoted love to

CHAPTER FIVE: Jesus Led With Love

Israel. Despite Israel's unfaithfulness, God expressed His infinite love for His people, all the more through love poetry, painting a beautiful imagery of God's extreme devotion and affection towards His Bride, the Church.

But then, love is also an action. That is why, in literary circles, it is characterized as an *active verb*. *"But God demonstrates His own love toward us, in that while we were still sinners, Christ died for us." (Rom. 5:8).* Love is not merely a feeling. Love is also an action, one that God shows from the very beginning of time. Out of His love, God established a rescue plan for humanity in the wake of Adam and Eve's fall. He told the serpent, *"And I will put enmity Between you and the woman, And between your seed and her Seed; He shall bruise your head, And you shall bruise His heel." (Genesis 3:15).* Out of His great love, God freed Israel from slavery in Egypt. He did not do this because they earned it, but because they were His people. Out of His love, God became fully *human*, yet fully *God* through the person of Jesus Christ, who lived a perfect life and died a death we deserved so that we could be restored to a right relationship with God. In each scenario, all of God's actions toward His people are motivated by nothing but pure love. He doesn't just say He loves us. He actually demonstrates that love. By coming into the world and sacrificing his own life for us, Jesus demonstrated the ultimate love of God. He died for us because He considered us friends worth dying for. *"No longer do I call you servants, for a servant does not know what his master is doing; but I have called you friends, for all things that I heard from My Father I have made known to you." (John 15:15).* This is radical love. It is the love that Jesus demonstrated during his time on Earth, and still demonstrates today, even if we fail see it the same way we see the love of our friends and family. In the final analysis, Jesus really does love us, not because of anything we have done, but because of who He is.

Jesus' love is loyal love. It is the kind of love we can depend on. When we long for love, what we are really longing for is the affection of unconditional love. Affection can come and go, and it doesn't satisfy our innate need to be loved without condition. What we really want is a *loyal affection* that is not driven by strict or begrudging obligation, but by deep compassion. When we treat someone as a close friend or family member, doing what is necessary to ensure their well-being and the health of the relationship, we can call that an act of affectionate love. While the action may be an obligation or duty, that sort of genuine, affectionate love also refers to the emotional motivation of love that drives overabundant expressions of generosity and care. This sort of affection assumes a pre-existing relationship, and it refers to actions that demonstrate loyalty to that relationship; to preserve and protect it and allow it to flourish. This type of affection also describes a posture in the relationship that can be expressed through many different acts. The Bible offers us a few examples of this sort of affectionate love. Jacob demanded this sort of affectionate love from his sons by extracting their promise to bury him in his homeland, which would require an entire pilgrimage out of Egypt. "When the time drew near that Israel must die, he called his son Joseph and said to him, *"Now if I have found favor in your sight, please put your hand under my thigh, and deal kindly and truly with me. Please do not bury me in Egypt, but let me lie with my fathers; you shall carry me out of Egypt and bury me in their burial place." And he said, "I will do as you have said." Then he said, "Swear to me." And he swore to him. So Israel bowed himself on the head of the bed."* (Gen. 47-31). Ruth was an immigrant. She lost her husband and children, but decides to stay committed to her mother-in-law. That was an act of genuine, affectionate love. *"Entreat me not to leave you, Or to turn back from following after you; For wherever you go, I will go; And wherever you lodge, I will lodge; Your people shall be my people, And your God, my God. Where you die, I will die, And there will I be buried. The Lord do*

CHAPTER FIVE: Jesus Led With Love

so to me, and more also, If anything but death parts you and me." (Ruth 1:16-17).

In order to truly love someone, there can be no prejudice or bias. Just because we disagree with a person's decisions, or choices, for that matter, doesn't mean we still can't love them. Jesus' love was unconditional and included all people, regardless of their background, ethnicity, or mistakes they might have made in life. The word *tolerance* is a commonly used one in today's world. While we must demonstrate a certain level of tolerance in our dealings with people, that does not translate to tolerance of any and all types of lifestyle. When a woman was caught in the act of adultery, Jesus did not condemn her. However, He did warn her to, *"Go and sin no more."* The Bible shares with us that Jesus was extremely compassionate with, and sympathetic to, the plight of all mankind. In many more instances than one, we can recall from the pages of the Bible that He was found in the company of the distraught and the marginalized. His disciples experienced moments of trepidation in which they felt compelled to protect Jesus from the crowds that He Himself openly welcomed. *"But when the multitudes knew it, they followed Him; and He received them and spoke to them about the Kingdom of God, and healed those who had need of healing. When the day began to wear away, the twelve came and said to Him, send the multitude away, that they may go into the surrounding towns and country, and lodge and get provisions, for we are in a deserted place here. But He said to them; You give them something to eat." (Lk 9: 11-13A).*

No matter the seemingly unsafe circumstances, Jesus was always empathetic to people, desiring to ease their pain as much as He could. We must never forget that He was also an emotional man, as He cried on more than one occasion. Admittedly, there were times when the crowds were only following Him for what He could give, but there definitely were people who followed Him because they wanted to hear what He had to say. *"And He came down with them and stood on a level place with a crowd of His disciples and a great multitude of people from all Judea and Jerusalem, and from the seacoast of Tyre and Sidon, who came to hear Him and be healed of their diseases." (Lk 6: 17)*. What is utterly fascinating about Him was that He didn't wait for people to come to Him. Jesus was always on the move, looking to alleviate distress and human suffering wherever He could find it. *"Then Jesus went about all the cities and villages, teaching in their synagogues, preaching the gospel of the Kingdom, and healing every sickness and every disease among the people. But when He saw the multitudes, He was moved with compassion for them, because they were weary and scattered, like sheep having no shepherd. Then He said to His disciples; The harvest truly is plentiful, but the laborers are few. Therefore pray the Lord of the harvest to send out laborers into His harvest." (Mt 9: 35-37)*. Jesus was alluding to the fact that each one of us must possess a humble spirit, and the mindset to be willing to place the needs of others above ours. Unconditional love has servanthood as its bedrock. Jesus was the perfect epitome of any principle He sought to teach. Aside from His crucifixion on the cross, the Master performed one of the most unselfish acts anyone could perform for a fellow human being. *"Jesus knowing that the Father had given all things into His hands, and that He had come from God and was going to God, rose from supper and laid aside His garments, took a towel and girded Himself. After that, He poured water into a basin and began to wash the disciples' feet, and to wipe them with the towel with which He was girded........So when He had washed their feet, taken His garments, and sat down again, He said to them: Do you know what I have done to you? You call Me Teacher and Lord, and you say well, for so I am. If I then, your Lord and Teacher, have washed your feet, you also ought to wash one another's feet. For I have given you an example, that you should do as I have done to you." (Jn 13: 2-5; 12-15).*

What makes this act of love even more profound is that He also washed the feet of Judas, who was present in the room, and had not yet departed to go and execute his act of betrayal. One can only imagine the thoughts that might have preoccupied Judas' mind at the time, knowing fully well that he was on the verge of betraying Jesus. Yet, Jesus had taught the same principle of accommodation on a previous occasion. *"But I say to you who hear: love your enemies, do good to those who hate you, bless those who curse you, and pray for those who spitefully use you." (Lk 6: 27-28).* The modern day believer would say, "You are really asking a lot Jesus!" Yet, He never taught anything He was not willing to model for those who followed Him. There were instances in which He knew His life might be in jeopardy, but He always felt that the needs of others was of greater importance. Lazarus had died. It was common knowledge that the Jews in Judea were plotting to kill Jesus. Nonetheless, He went back to Judea, in full cognizance of the fact that Lazarus was a part of His assignment.

That is what genuine love does. It drives one to become selfless. Each one of us must take inventory as to whether we are really walking in unconditional love, or whether our love is based upon what others first do for us. Many marriages suffer because, singularly or jointly, the demonstration of love by one party to the union is predicated upon what the other party gives. There is no way any of us can properly love at that level without the abiding presence of the Holy Spirit. The greatest dimension, and the greatest manifestation, of love is forgiveness. Imagine the hordes of relationships that have been destroyed because forgiveness eludes the heart of so many people. Ultimately, an unforgiving heart and spirit leads to bitterness. An inability to love at that level is indicative of a believer who has not fully surrendered to the

Lordship of Christ. It is astounding to think that Jesus even forgave the people who crucified Him. *"And when they had come to the place called Calvary, there they crucified Him, and the criminals, one on the right hand and the other on the left. Then Jesus said: Father, forgive them, for they do not know what they do." (Lk 23: 33-34).*

This act of forgiveness must count as the most emotive moment of human accommodation in all of human history. Jesus had just been beaten beyond recognition. He had just been humiliated by being spat upon. At that poignant moment, blood was running profusely down his body, and life was slowly ebbing out of Him. Yet, He still found sufficient strength to delve into His wellspring of love to forgive. More often than not, we want others to make sacrifices for us, but are unwilling to reciprocate the gesture. Even though we are not called to die on a cross for others, there still should be a willingness to sacrifice for others whenever it is necessary. Also, our motivation for helping others should not be because we seek applause. Love is an action word. *"By this we know love, because He laid down His life for us. And we also ought to lay down our lives for the brethren. But whoever has this world's goods, and sees his brother in need, and shuts up his heart from him, how does the love of God abide in him? My little children, let us not love in word or in tongue, but in deed and in truth." (1 Jn 3: 16-18).* Jesus genuinely loved everyone. Without doubt, most of us have encountered people who claim that they love everyone, only for us to quickly discover that they have biases and prejudices that they are perfectly unwilling to jettison. *Racism, sexism,* and *classism* are a few of the mindsets that largely separate us, and they are just as prevalent amongst Christians as they are in secular society. The old saying is that *"eleven o'clock on a Sunday morning is the most segregated time in America."* Yet those same people herald the fact that they love the Lord with all of their heart, and while that may sound good to the proclaimer, it is not very factual in practice.

Through the benefit of my privilege as a Christian minister over the years, I have observed that this is not just an ideology that exists only in the pews. It has also taken root amongst the leadership. Scripture is very clear about the fact that we are supposed to be the example. *"Let no man despise your youth, but be an example to the believers in word, in conduct, in love, in spirit, in faith, in purity." (1 Tim 4: 12).* No one has greater justification for retaliation for how He was treated than Jesus. Yet, at no time did He ever allow His maltreatment to affect His approach to life and ministry. We often offer excuses for ourselves on the rather convenient, though totally misguided platitude that we can indulge in the luxury of disallowing others to take advantage of us. However, scripture is clear on the point that you can only be offended if you allow yourself to be. *"Great peace have they who love Your law, and nothing shall offend them." (Ps 119: 165).* What an awesome proclamation! The Bible says that if you are anchored in the *Word*, you will not be offended. The lyrics of a popular church song goes thus, *"If I hold my peace and let the Lord fight my battle, victory shall be mine!"* This sounds both wonderful and ideal in principle until it's time to put it into practice. As you read this book, I urge you to take personal inventory of where you are in your love walk, especially if you are a leader. You simply cannot take others where you do not, either by acts of omission or commission, tread yourself. One hastens to admit that this proposition is not always humanly easy, particularly if you have been deeply wounded by someone who is unrepentant. In scriptural truth, however, this has nothing to do with you. The negativity thrown your way by others has nothing to do with how you elect to respond. It also pays to remember that forgiveness is not for the ultimate benefit of the other person, but for you. Time and again, Jesus was deprecated and insulted by being labeled a devil, a drunk, a heretic, and any other such fanciful name His traducers could conjure in their misguided imagination. He remained unfazed by all they said. For the man or woman who has been truly transformed by the renewing of their mind, you should be doing your utmost best to bring about restoration and reconciliation in relationships. This, of course, means that we have to die to ourselves. The apostle Paul said, *"I die daily."* He also said the love of God always served to constrain him. Jesus said, *"do unto others as you would have them to do unto you."* The application of these principles takes relevance not only with people in your congregation or your immediate family. They seek application with all of mankind. Our world is filled with people who are hurting and struggling on daily basis. In the position that the Lord has placed me as His humble servant in ministry, I am exposed to the opportunity to speak with people who are often at their wits end. Almost always, all they are looking for is someone; just about anyone, to care.

I have been blessed with the opportunity to travel extensively across the United Stares, and to many other countries, and in the course of these travels, I have encountered some of the most devastating situations imaginable. I have found people in circumstances that brought tears to my eyes. I have found myself giving away my clothes, and emptying my pockets of all that I had, in the knowledge that, although I couldn't help everybody, at the very least, I helped somebody. I urge you to always keep in mind that your worst is someone else's best. Our love for one another must remain consistent and unwavering. There was never a time when the Master failed to demonstrate love and compassion. Even in some of the most horrible circumstances, He still lavished His love upon whoever needed it; whether it was a crowd or one person. I can see someone forgivably throwing up his hands in despair, and saying, *"Well, when is enough just enough? Aren't there some people simply waiting to take advantage of me?"* My response is simple. That may well be true. Yet, not everyone

CHAPTER FIVE: Jesus Led With Love

is dishonorable. We ought not to penalize that person who is in desperate need of help simply because of the lack of integrity of another individual. Recently, my wife and I watched a movie about a school that was about to shut down their music program because of lack of funding. The teacher who had taught music at the school for twenty years would also lose his job, a situation that was especially disruptive because his wife was pregnant. Another teacher in the school took a special interest in the situation, even though he wasn't connected to the music program at all. That other teacher started taking professional martial arts classes so that he could compete in a tournament, win prize money, and hopefully donate it to save the music program, and most importantly, save the music teacher'sjob. He wasn't particularly good at martial arts, and initially took terrible beatings. Yet, he was willing to risk his life to save someone else's. The long and short of the story was that he won all the money necessary to save the music program. Tragically, however, the school treasurer embezzled all of the money. That, thankfully, was not the end of the story. The organization on whose platform he took part in the competition learnt about what he was trying to accomplish, and gave the school more than enough to save the program. This is the love of God in action. This teacher had no stake whatsoever in the survival of the program, but he was concerned about the plight of his fellow teacher and the students.

When we demonstrate the love of God, we realize that it's better to give than to receive. The legacy of Jesus Christ is love. It is a lesson that every believer must learn. Let's face it, it can only be a matter of sad commentary that, while God asks that the pillars of His church be built with love, and with the fabric of kindness, men bring stones. I will explain. A cathedral, by its pre-eminent status as the principal church building that accommodates the episcopal presence of a Bishop, is a grand and statuesque structure. It is usually constructed with such scrupulous attention to architectural detail that its magnificence and splendor is nothing short of a glorious monument to the awesome might of God. That may well be all true. Yet, authentic glorification of God rests, not on the massive pillars, marble floors, richly-upholstered vestries, expansive aisles, stately pulpit and picturesque frescoes of the cathedral. The real structure of the church will have to find a resting place in the fabric of love that ought to be woven into the totality of the existence of the cathedral as a place of worship of an awesome God. Indeed, it is not just about coming to beautifully decorated buildings with all of the modern high-tech equipment. Believe it or not, many people may come to the building lavishly dressed, and driving the finest of cars, yet are internally hurting, and very badly, for that matter. They come in hurting, and all too often, they leave the same way because they have learned how to mask their pain or, at the very best, they receive something that is nothing more than a band aid on a broken arm. Jesus never had a problem with touching others, just as He never had a problem with allowing others to touch Him. *"When they had crossed over, they came to the land of Gennesaret. And when the men of that place recognized Him, they sent out into all that surrounding region, brought to Him all that were sick, and begged Him that they might only touch the hem of His garment. And as many as touched it were made perfectly well."* (Mt 14: 34-36). We have lost our sense of unity and community. Each one of us has the gift of love that can be freely given to others. Freely you have received. Freely you must give.

Prayer of Focus

My Lord and Savior, I accept that I was created out of love, and that from love I came, and to love I shall return. May my love for others kindle flames of joy and hope in them. May the light and warmth of Your grace inspire me to follow the way of The Lord and Master, Jesus Christ. Give me grace to use my love to serve you in your Kingdom, now and forever. Bless me with love, Almighty God, that I may love as you love, and such that I may continue to show patience, kindness, tolerance, caring and love to others. In Jesus name. Amen.

CHAPTER SIX

Jesus Led By Faith

"And He said to her, "Daughter, your faith has made you well. Go in peace, and be healed of your affliction." (Mk 5:34)

At the very core of all Christian values and beliefs is the element of faith. Not surprisingly, when most people speak of faith, they tend to allude only to that which is spiritual. Yet, I am of the informed opinion that each one of us has faith, regardless of whether we are fundamentally of a spiritual bent of mind or not. After all, we can arrive at a building and take a seat, with the "faith" that the chair we are about to sit on will support us. Diners arrive at a restaurant, order a meal, and eat without a second thought. They do so without morbidly dwelling on the possibility that there might be contaminants in the food. Invariably, this is a reflection of the unwavering "faith" they have in the name brand of the dining establishment.

Having established the basic universality of faith in our everyday existence, we are yet compelled to delve into the deeper meaning of faith as it relates to the realm of the spiritual. *"Now the just shall live by faith; but if anyone draws back, My soul has no pleasure in him." (Heb 10:38).* Living by faith means to believe in advance that which only makes sense in the reverse. I wouldn't be surprised if your instant query were, *"Shouldn't everything make sense?"* My response would be, *"Things might be expected to make sense, or to be perfectly logical, so to speak, in the natural world. But God is not constrained to logicality. In other words, He is not trying to make sense. Rather, He is trying to make faith."* All that Noah had was the promise of God that it was going to rain. He had to transform that statement into his mantra, and the consuming reason for his very existence. Each day of his life, and for the next one hundred and twenty years, Noah knew exactly what his agenda was. Let us attempt to observe this scenario through the lens of our western understanding, and make some sense of the seeming ludicrousness of Noah's mission. Surely, it must rank as sheer insanity that we would attempt to build a boat in the middle of nowhere, especially with no sight of water as far as the eyes can see. Since the average person does not want to be thought as having taken leave of his senses, wits and faculties, only ridicule, embarrassment, and shame would probably be all that might attend such an enterprise in perceived stupidity. However, the one thing that runs like a recurring decimal through the Old Testament is the sort of aggressive faith that is a rarity in today's body of believers.

The Old Testament is a study in the fortitude borne of unflinching faith. Savage adversities, tumultuous storms, and even imminent death, seemed to pose no threat to these men and women who were only too willing to trust God with their very life. *"Though He slay me, yet will I trust Him. Even so, I will defend my own ways before Him. He also shall be my salvation, for a hypocrite could not come before Him. (Job 13: 15-16).* In the full knowledge that to unceremoniously arrive at the king's presence without a formal invitation could only spell certain and summary death, Esther was still willing to put her life on the line for the protection of her

CHAPTER SIX: Jesus Led By Faith

people. *"Go, gather all the Jews who are present in Shushan, and fast for me; neither eat nor drink for three days, night or day. My maids and I will fast likewise. And so I will go to the king, which is against the law; and if I perish, I perish!"* (Esther 4: 16).

Again, faith is a word that is commonly used, but not always understood. Some of that confusion comes from the many different ways the word "faith" is used in everyday conversation. For instance, the word faith is commonly used to refer to belief in something, despite lacking any evidence for it. Ultimately, what is important is what the Bible means by faith. The closest that the Bible comes to offering an exact definition of faith is in Heb 11:1, *"Now faith is the assurance of things hoped for, the conviction of things not seen."* This passage alludes to the central feature of faith as being *confidence* or *trust*. In the Bible, the object of faith is God and His promises. A clear example of this is seen in Abraham's encounter with God in Genesis 15. In response to God's promise of countless descendants, Abraham *"believed in the Lord, and He accounted it to him for righteousness."* (Gen 15:6). The Apostle Paul's comments on Abraham's faith are instructive. *"He did not waver at the promise of God through unbelief, but was strengthened in faith, giving glory to God, and being fully convinced that what He had promised He was also able to perform."* (Rom 4:20-21). Thus, faith means putting your trust in God and having confidence that He will fulfill His promises.

Also, faith is more than *intellectual assurance.* Imagine you were witnessing a tightrope walker pushing a wheelbarrow across the rope, high above the Niagara Falls. After watching him go back and forth several times, he asks for a volunteer to sit in the wheelbarrow as he pushes it across the falls. It is one thing to *believe* that he can successfully push you across the rope over the falls. That is faith at an intellectual level. It is, however, an entirely different proposition to actually get in the wheelbarrow, and entrust yourself to the tightrope walker. That is *faith* at the biblical level. This is the sort of genuine biblical faith that expresses itself in everyday life. *"Thus also faith by itself, if it does not have works, is dead." (James 2:17).* Faith works through love to produce tangible evidence of its existence in a person's life. Expressed differently, the obedience that pleases God comes from faith, rather than a mere sense of duty or obligation. Lere's face it, there is a world of difference between the husband who buys his wife flowers out of genuine delight, and one who buys them simply and merely out of a sense of duty. Faith is so important because it is the means by which we have a relationship with God. *"For by grace you have been saved through faith, and that not of yourselves; it is the gift of God." (Eph 2:8).* Faith is how we receive the benefits of what Jesus has done for us. He lived a life of perfect obedience to God for *our* sake. He died to pay the penalty for *our* sinful rebellion against God. He rose from the dead to defeat sin, death, and the devil. The least we can do is place our faith, totally and unequivocally, in Him, and by doing so, we receive forgiveness for our sins and the gift of eternal life. Conclusively, therefore, faith means relying completely on who Jesus is and what He has done to be made right with God.

Let us take our study of faith even closer to Jesus. When faith is alive in a person's life, it becomes a catalyst for a life bereft of fear. Jesus presents us with a perfect template for living such a life. He was never limited by any type of inhibition or fear. His faith was totally anchored in His heavenly Father. He was and is a man who was totally surrendered to the plan of God, not only for Himself but for all of mankind. *"For as by one man's disobedience many were made sinners, so also by one Man's obedience many will be made righteous." (Rom 5: 19).* The twelve disciples were often beleaguered in trying to explain away many of the things they observed

CHAPTER SIX: Jesus Led By Faith

Jesus do. While they were correct in ascribing these feats to a man, Jesus was decidedly not just any man. I have often found myself wondering just what type of child Jesus might have been. Did He perform any miracles as a child? At His first recorded miracle, at the wedding at Cana of Galilee, His mother told the servants to do whatever He told them to do. From what level of understanding was she making that statement? The memories of the encounter that she and her husband, Joseph, had with Him in Jerusalem had to still be lingering with her. Jesus had very clearly, and in both succinct and unambiguous terms, advised his earthly parents that He must be about His Father's business. *"Then He went down with them and came to Nazareth, and was subject to them, but His mother kept all these things in her heart."* *(Lk 2: 51).* When believers are without faith, or have limited faith, it is inevitable that much of what the Lord wants to accomplish through them will never come to fruition. While one can only marvel at how everything Jesus said manifested immediately, what is both mind boggling and confounding is that there was never a time when He entertained thoughts of doubt or worry. Quite often, His question to potential candidates for a miracle was, *"Do you believe that I can do this?"* When the reply was in the affirmative, His answer was, *"Your faith has made you whole!"* We should note that He did not just say one's faith has made one well, but *whole*. According to Webster's dictionary, *whole* means, *"containing all the elements properly belonging; complete; nothing missing; nothing lacking."*

Whilst He was here on Earth, Jesus entrusted His entire life onto His Father's hands. At no time did He attempt to wrest Himself away from the Father. In keeping with that thought, there were instances when He stated to the Father in prayer that He fully entrusted the moment onto His hands, yet needed visible proof for those who were observing Him.

"Then they took away the stone from the place where the dead man was lying. And Jesus lifted up His eyes and said, Father, I thank You that You have heard Me, but because of the people who are standing by I said this, that they may believe that You sent Me." (Jn 11: 41-42). The life of faith is undoubtedly one of a transformative journey. How Jesus lived His life during His own era was a tremendous challenge for those who were not accustomed to such radical thinking. One of the dangers of watching someone perform miracles is that a person's faith can get lost in the *person* and the *miracle*, as opposed to desiring a relationship with the *source* of the wonder itself. Scripture is quite clear that Jesus, to mitigate the tendency of observers elevating Him to a pedestal of awesome hero worship, never accepted credit for anything He did. He always ceded the glory to the Father. *"Do you not believe that I am in the Father, and the Father in Me? The words that I speak to you I do not speak on My own authority, but the Father who dwells in Me does the works." (Jn 14: 10).*

In the course of my own journey, I have learned that living by faith is not, and will never be, an easy enterprise. This becomes especially true when extraneous influences come to bear upon the circumstances you may be facing at any given moment. The temptation is always to attempt to find a solution to the problem on your own without any assistance from the Lord. Additionally, we also often misguidedly feel that some situations are too trivial to "trouble" God with. No such notion, of course, could be more absurd. We must live in the wisdom that there is nothing too small, nor too great, to merit the loving attention of our Heavenly Father. As a leader, there are times when I have found myself in the classic eleventh hour situation, in which I dared not proceed without divine intervention. In such situations, intellect will fall far short of the mark. There is simply no way we can apply earthly solutions to heavenly matters. Jesus spent enormous

CHAPTER SIX: Jesus Led By Faith

amounts of time querying the Father as to how He was to handle all of the various illnesses, diseases, sicknesses, and socio-religious matters He was confronted with on daily basis. Given that He set the standard, how can we even remotely entertain the thought of lowering that standard by even an iota? I marvel at the faith of Jesus, as there was not one situation that He was confronted with that He had to take a moment to step back from. Rather, He would plunge head long into whatever He was confronted with. This is nothing short of a statement of the depth of His faith. Far too many believers make statements of faith but have no real "depth" to their faith. Our heavenly Father is a God of *impossible possibilities.* I will explain.

Many of us waste our prayers on only that which is possible. There is no need to *waste* faith on that which is possible. Faith seeks challenge. That is why it is called *faith.* *"For the eyes of the Lord run to and fro throughout the whole earth, to show Himself strong on behalf of those whose heart is loyal to Him." (2 Chr 16: 9).* Unfortunately the orientation of the modern day church is such that the average believer has not been taught total *trust, reliance,* and *dependence* on God. We are not seekers of God and His divine power. In truth, we merely seek the superficial emotional thrill, which is fleeting at best. People come in through the door laden with their personal baggages and burdens, and leave exactly the same way. In sharp contrast, never was there a time when the shattered and broken came into Jesus's presence, and left the same way. *"Now Jesus called His disciples to Himself and said; I have compassion on the multitude, because they have now continued with Me three days and have nothing to eat, and I do not want to send them away hungry, lest they faint on the way." (Mt 15: 32).* This particular scenario led to the feeding of thousands of men, women, and children. Each person was able to eat as much as they wanted, with seven baskets left over. At another such occasion, twelve baskets were left over. These are simply amazing testimonies. Let us also be mindful of the fact that the "loaves" were only about the size of a hamburger bun. Also, we cannot miss the fact that after Jesus prayed over the fish and loaves the food multiplied in the disciples hands. As I meditated on that thought, I suddenly realized that, by now, the faith of the disciples would have *gone through the roof*. It could not have been otherwise after observing such an astounding miracle. However, that was not the case.

Even upto and after the Master's death there were still moments of consternation and doubt amongst the disciples. Prior to what we call *"The Great Commission,"* the disciples were deployed to minister to the masses with the same power that Jesus had demonstrated. The scriptures say that, although they rejoiced over what they were able to accomplish, their elation was short lived. *"Then the seventy returned with joy, saying; Lord, even the demons are subject to us in Your name." (Lk 10: 17)*. Truth be told, even in these times, many of us have experienced miracles so great they can only qualify as being beyond human comprehension and understanding. Yet, rather than those stupendous occurrences fueling our faith, our faith has remained stagnant. Quite often, I have had people ask me what happened to the *"greater"* that Jesus stated we would be able to accomplish. The stark truth is that the *"greater"* will never manifest if the people of God are not in possession of *"greater faith."* Think of the number of Christian ministries that appear to be going nowhere and doing nothing. This is as a result of stagnant leadership. Stagnant leadership, itself, can only produce stagnant faith in the led. Leadership in this culture is in dire need of men and women who are in possession of a *sure* and *strong* faith that will be the catalyst for the supernatural power that is desperately needed to contend with, and to combat the demonic forces that oppose members of the Body of Christ. There is currently a leadership vacuum that looks nothing like what Jesus modeled whilst He was still with us. Today's church appears to be merely on the lookout for leaders who hand out band aids and tourniquets every week, in the tragic process offering no viable cures or solutions for the more distressing aspects of the Christian pilgrim's journey. What is of far graver issue is that the people of God, in blissful ignorance, accept it as being quality leadership. The people of the New Testament era followed Jesus because they knew that the quality of their life would improve immensely, even with the briefest of encounters with Him. Our current experience is that the faithful chase after their favorite preacher all over the country, not because of any demonstration of substantial spiritual power, but because of his or her charisma, a culture that entices us to perfect our "brand," rather than perfecting our faith.

Living by faith carries with it a dimension of life in which we voluntarily relinquish control and allow God to guide us at all times. As I stated previously, Jesus never boasted of an original thought. Rather, He constantly sought His Father for instruction and direction. Our current Babylonian way of life has so impacted our society and culture that many believers have been swayed in their allegiance, in much the same way that Adam and Eve were drawn away from their primordial fealty to God. Faith is a dimension that is supposed to transcend our cultural norms and beliefs. Our enemy's avowed intention is to make us forget all about God, and attempt to get all that we desire through our own human efforts. Personally, I have learned that those efforts are ineffectual at best, and futile at worst. Most of us are ultimately duped into thinking that we have become successful through our own efforts. Sadly, we only end up enjoying mild success compared to what the Lord had originally planned for us. *"There is a way that seems right to a man, but its end is the way of death." (Prov 14: 12).* I am perennially stymied by the ignorance of some of God's people, who see the life of faith as one of fantasy; that believing God to do the impossible is beyond the realm of reality. The irony is that despite the fact that we cannot see our kidney or our bladder, we believe that they are there, and that they are heroically performing their assigned physiological functions. To all intent and purposes, such faithlessness ought to merely classify one as an *"unbelieving believer,"* if there is such a thing. As a believer in the Lord Jesus Christ, the supernatural ought to be effortlessly natural for us. If we cannot trust God by simple faith, then our ritual attendance at church services is nothing but a waste of our time. We might as well remain at home, or go fishing, instead. Why continue to listen to messages about this amazing God if we don't believe that He is capable of doing amazing things through His people? The lyrics of a very popular gospel song says, *"An incredible God deserves incredible praise!"*

As I write these words, I can think of the numerous times in my life wherein, were it not for my faith in God, I couldn't possibly have accomplished anything of substantial value, be it in my calling as a minister of His Word, or in the more seemingly mundane aspects of life. Be it as it may that we might fervently hearken to our Lord's command to live by faith, there will still be, most definitely for that matter, daunting challenges that will sorely test that faith. However, the grand utility of our faith is that it will accord us the spiritual privilege of not seeing those challenges as insurmountable problems, but as mere opportunities to *act* like God. I hasten to crave your understanding that I do not imply that you *become* God, which is both inconceivable and impossible, but to *act* like Him. We are created in His image and likeness, therefore we also carry His DNA. No matter how long, or how hard we scour the scriptures, we will never encounter a narrative in which Jesus was ever in a quandary as to what to do next. Additionally, it becomes imperative that leaders in the Body of Christ exemplify great

CHAPTER SIX: Jesus Led By Faith

faith in the presence of their fellow workers in the Lord's vineyard. It must not be forgotten that, in any congregation of believers, there will be those that have faith, and there will be those that do not have faith. I pointed out previously how Jesus had twelve men who *walked* and *worked* closely with Him. Yet, we notice that He did not have Thomas as one of them, especially when more intimate contact was needed. Thomas was a dedicated and brave follower of Jesus, and would later help spread His gospel across the world. Yet, Thomas would later gain greater renown for his reaction after Jesus' resurrection. While the other apostles believed Mary about the resurrection, Thomas didn't initially believe. This instance is where he got the nickname, *"Doubting Thomas."* The resurrected Christ went to the Upper Room to visit with his apostles and followers. Thomas was notably absent from this event because he didn't believe. He said, *"............Unless I see in His hands the print of the nails, and put my finger into the print of the nails, and put my hand into His side, I will not believe." (John 20:23).* Eight days later, Thomas had the opportunity to see the marks of the nails, and put his hand into His side. He fell to his knees at Jesus' feet, and said, *"My Lord and my God!"* While he had doubted before seeing, Thomas makes this declaration of Jesus' divinity, something that is important to have in the scriptural account of the resurrection. In fact, Thomas' declaration of Jesus' divinity is the first account recorded in the scriptures. Thomas' reaction after the resurrection is what he's most known for as an apostle, despite many instances of being a loyal follower of Jesus.

Leaders must also guard against adopting other people's fears as their own. When Jesus decided to visit his sick friend, Lazarus, in Judea, it was at a time when Jesus was despised by the authorities in Jerusalem for His miracles and teachings. Therefore, it was considered dangerous for Him to come so close to potential hostility. The apostles were afraid that Jesus would be stoned, but Thomas; the same latter-day Doubting Thomas, showed his bravery and dedication to Jesus. *"Let us also go, that we may die with him." (John 11:16)*. After this faithful declaration, all of the apostles joined Jesus on the journey to Judea where Jesus later raised Lazarus from the dead. What is significant here is that Jesus proceeded, undaunted by the spirit of fear that surrounded Him while on His way to the tomb of Lazarus. Just imagine the type of faith that it takes to *walk* on water, and then to *stand* on water as He lifted Peter up when he sank because of his lack of faith. Let us also pay heed to the fact that Jesus' rebuke of Peter wasn't quite as stern as when He rebuked them when they were on the ship and Jesus calmed the storm. At that time He said, "Why did you have *no faith!*" However, to Peter He said, "O you of *little faith,* why did you doubt?" (Mt 14: 31). My thought is that, at least, Peter exhibited the faith to get out of the boat and take steps on the water until he began to question his own faith. Through the years I have observed so many people that were destined for greatness but couldn't get out of their own way to trust God to use them to do miraculous things while here on Earth.

I dare say that a great portion of the Body of Christ do not realize that our life and destiny is actually in our own hands. For decades we have been taught to think that everything rests on God, and that we have no responsibility whatsoever as to how our life will play out. Were matters quite as simple and prosaic as that, the Lord would not have seen it fit to give us free will. Every individual, whether saved or unsaved, is a steward of their own life. A person's decision can either result in a life of utopia, or one of despair. An interaction with many an incarcerated man or woman will reveal that it was just one fateful decision that landed them where they are. When you couple our power of impactful personal decision with our choice of who we allow to influence us as we

CHAPTER SIX: Jesus Led By Faith

make our journey through life, you have the perfect recipe for either potential disaster or a wholesome life of joy and abundance. *"A wise man will hear and increase learning, and a man of understanding will attain wise counsel." (Prov 1: 5).* I truly believe that the inalienable obligation of each one of us is to unlearn much of the errant religious teaching we have received, and which has done us the tragic disfavor of watering down our faith. No one needs faith to do *nothing*. That statement might appear a little absurd. What I imply is that multitudes are doing *nothing* that resembles the pursuit of destiny. Jesus said, *"I must work the works of Him who sent Me while it is day, the night is coming when no one can work." (Jn 9: 4).* Nothing should give greater tranquility than to know that our faith in God supplies the reassurance that we are always going to be taken care of; that we are never alone. Our heavenly Father states that He will never leave us nor forsake us. For just about anything that He leads us into, He has already planned a glorious solution, if only because it is all for His glory. The apostle Paul punctuates that thought by letting us know that God cannot deny Himself. *"If we are faithless, He remains faithful; He cannot deny Himself." (2 Tim 2:13).* I am of the conviction that so much more could occur for most of us if we would only rely fully on God. Life is not the bewildering maze that some of us have made it to be. Once again, I am pained to point to how so many miss the humanity of Jesus, and only picture God dressed up in an earthly suit. When we live by faith, the supernatural becomes our reality, a dimension that very few venture into. Enter by the narrow gate; for wide is the gate and broad is the way that leads to destruction. Many of us insist on entering through the wide gate of perdition. *"Narrow is the gate and difficult is the way which leads to life, and there are few who find it." (Mt 7: 13-14).*

The enemy of our soul will always attempt to superimpose his thoughts upon us, desiring to get us to either question

God's word to us, or to doubt ourselves. Greatness lies at the core of every man or woman that the Lord has ever created. It is sad to think of the billions of people who have lived and died with magnificent gifts and talents that were never shared with the world. Dr Myles Munroe once said that the greatest resource on earth is not the oil fields of Kuwait, or the gold mines of Algeria, or the diamond mines of South Africa. The richest resource on planet Earth today, he said, is the graveyard. Untold reservoirs of undeveloped and unexploited human potential lie in the graveyard because of people who never possessed the *faith* to plumb the depths of their being. Cures for diseases, beautiful architectural edifices, stirring poems, soulful songs, and uplifting sermons are just a few of the wonders that the world never experienced because of lack of faith. We thank God for Jesus. The Bible even says about Him that He did so much that there are not enough libraries to contain the books that would be written about all that He performed. Indeed, there are also many other things that Jesus did which, if they were written down, one after the other, even the entire world itself could not possibly contain the books that would be written. *Amen.* Let us look at all that Jesus was able to accomplish in just thirty three years. Could it be that the only reason why you are unable to unlock the plethora of magnificent gifts accorded you at birth is because of your lack of faith in God, and your lack of confidence in yourself? Even more tragic, there is another group of people who are waiting on someone else to give them permission to live. Be very careful, then, how you live, *"not as unwise but as wise, making the most of every opportunity, because the days are evil." (Eph 5: 15-16 (NIV).* Each one of us has been given a measure of faith, and that faith can be increased. What fascinates me is that the power of God was still at work in Jesus even as He hung on the cross. He invited one of the thieves into paradise with Him, forgave the people that crucified Him, made sure that His mother was taken care of before His departure, and fulfilled every scripture written about Him. None of us has a plausible excuse for not fulfilling the plan of God for our life. Jesus Christ perfectly executed the Father's plan to the letter, and left on record for us what it looks like to live a life of faith. Not one person that ever came into His presence could ever say that they did not see faith on display. Now, it is our turn to replicate His life of faith in our own lives.

Prayer of Focus

Lord, open my mouth to 'Ask.' Allow me to be absolutely clear about my desire, for in

this clarity lies my faith to receive. Lord, open my mind to 'Believe' that I have already received, and that what I want is unquestionably mine, for this is unwavering faith in operation. Lord, open my heart and hands to 'Receive.' I ask. I believe. I receive. I am receiving now. I am receiving all that is good for my life now. My faith is like night driving. My headlights will pick only the two hundred feet in front of me. Yet, I will reach my destination. I do not have to see the entire distance ahead. I trust. I believe. I will receive. In Jesus Name. Amen.

CHAPTER SEVEN
Jesus Led With Emotional Intelligence

"For we do not have a High Priest who cannot sympathize with our weaknesses, but was in all points tempted as we are, yet without sin." (Heb 4:15)

Emotional intelligence is a crucial aspect of effective leadership. It involves the ability to recognize, understand, manage, and use emotions in oneself, and in others. Not surprisingly, most people tend to confuse *emotional intelligence* with *empathy*, if not even conflate the two concepts. That, of course, is also because *emotional intelligence* and *empathy* are closely related and often used interchangeably. However, they are not the same thing. While emotional intelligence refers to *the ability to identify, understand, and manage one's own emotions and the emotions of others,* empathy specifically refers to *the ability to understand and share the feelings of another person.*

The key components of emotional intelligence are *self-awareness, self-regulation, motivation, empathy,* and *social skills.* People with high emotional intelligence are able to recognize their own emotions and the impact they have on others. They are also able to regulate their emotions in a healthy manner, rather than allowing their feelings to control their behavior. Additionally, they are not only able to understand and empathize with the emotions of others, they also possess the strong social skills that enable them to build and maintain positive relationships. Clearly, the strongest component of emotional intelligence is empathy, which is *the ability to understand and share the feelings of another person.* It involves putting yourself in someone else's shoes and seeing things from their perspective, which is why empathy allows us to connect with others on a truly profound level, to feel their pain or joy, and to respond in a way that is appropriate and helpful for their current circumstances.

Therefore, empathy and emotional intelligence are closely related. People with high emotional intelligence are often quite empathetic, as they are able to understand and share the emotions of others. To stretch definitions even further, empathy is a key component of *social skills,* which are an important aspect of emotional intelligence. Social skills involve the ability to communicate effectively, build and maintain relationships, and resolve conflicts. People with high emotional intelligence are able to regulate their own emotions in a healthy way, which allows them to be more empathetic towards others. They are able to recognize their own emotions and understand how they impact others, which makes them more attuned to the emotions of others. Jesus possessed a high index of emotional intelligence. He had genuine empathy. He was adroit at social skills.

A fundamental pillar of emotional intelligence is *self-awareness,* which involves recognizing one's own emotions, strengths, weaknesses, and their impact on others. Undoubtedly, Jesus was a man who maintained firm control of His emotions, even when He displayed sorrow or anger. Without doubt, a school of thought exists that believes that as soon as you display any degree of anger, you have lost control of your emotions, while the expression of sorrow is a sign of weakness. Yet, I am of the conviction that displaying these human emotions merely reveal the totality

CHAPTER SEVEN: Jesus Led With Emotional Intelligence

of the human experience. Many people cause themselves untold harm because they choose to stifle these emotions that were obviously given to us by our Creator when we were conceived. If Jesus had never displayed the full range of emotions that the average person goes through then He would have left us no hope as to how we could ever relate to Him. *"Be angry, and do not sin; do not let the sun go down on your wrath." (Eph 4: 26).*

We must handle our emotions in a self-regulatory manner. Asbelievers, we ought to always be under the control of the Holy Spirit. Yet, the scriptures, not grudgingly, make clear that while the spirit might be perfectly willing, the flesh is tragically weak. This is where Jesus demonstrated remarkable self-regulation skills, as He was never found at the extreme in any area of the human emotions. He cried like any other man. He was angry, like any other man. He was sorrowful, like any other man. He was compassionate, like any other man. He was joyful, like any other man, and He was in agony, like any other man. Yet, these human displays of emotion do not portray a man who was not in control of Himself, if only because in each moment, He was in complete control of His faculties. Quite often, the religious order of the day saw fit to accuse Him of being the devil, or at best being influenced by the devil. He never responded with violence or hostility. *"And the multitudes were amazed and sad. Could this be the Son of David? Now when the Pharisees heard it they said; This fellow does not cast out demons except by Beelzebub, the ruler of the demons." (Mt 12:23-24).* Rather than attempting to fight fire with fire, He was wise enough to respond with truth. *"But Jesus knew their thoughts, and said to them: Every kingdom divided against itself its brought to desolation, and every city or house divided against itself will not stand." (Mt 12: 25).* In today's world it is quite obvious that a great portion of the population is bent on resorting to extreme displays of violence at the slightest provocation.

We tend to resort to the most base of our human emotions to resolve our differences, without any forethought about it becoming a generational issue.

The ability to self-regulate oneself is the hallmark of *gentility*. I stand to be controverted that the Son of Man was the perfect gentleman. His disposition teaches us that true gentility is acquired through tremendous self-discipline, being a trait that comes to a man only after he has developed sufficient control over his negative passions. Show me a man who has achieved victory over vehemence, panic or resentment in the face of irritating or annoying circumstances, and I'll show you the perfect gentleman. I have always held the view that the brash and aggressive individual is an affront to any concept of the civil and cultivated mind, and that crudity in any form can only be an antithesis of what genuine spirituality stands for. Anyone who would lay a claim to the spiritual must be distinguishable by the sheer quality of his gentleness. A gentleman is a cultured man, since he exercises modesty and restraint in all things, with an ever-abiding consideration for the feelings and sensibilities of others. A perfect gentleman abhors and avoids discord in any form. He won't respond to a harsh word, either totally disregarding it, or meeting it with a contrastingly gentle word, in perfect tandem with what the Book of Life prescribes, *"A gentle answer turns away wrath, but a harsh word stirs up anger."* Such a man is indeed very wise, for while otherwise uncontrolled men continue to labor under the yoke of the strain of the needless upheavals and turbulence with which they torture themselves, he is calm and composed, qualities with which he goes ahead to confront and win the various battles of life.

Throughout time our heavenly Father has done nothing except to shower humanity with His unwavering love. Words escape me as I feebly attempt to even fathom the thought that He was only too willing to sacrifice His only Son as living atonement for the depravity and sin of the entire world. *"He*

CHAPTER SEVEN: Jesus Led With Emotional Intelligence

who did not spare His own Son, but delivered Him up for us all, how shall He not with Him also freely give us all things." *(Rom 8:32).* During His tenure on Earth, Jesus allowed Himself to be subjected to, and feel every type, and every level, of the human experience. *"For we do not have a High Priest who cannot sympathize with our weaknesses, but was in all points tempted as we are, yet without sin." (Heb 4:15).* There was never a time when He was not openly caring about the plight of those that chose to follow Him. His compassion was exemplary. It should be heartbreaking to those of us that profess to be believers in Christ Jesus as to how uncaring we have become as a society. We have entered the age of the *"selfie"!* Most people have more pictures of themselves on their phones than anyone else. People stop at any given moment to take a picture of themselves, a frivolous pastime that does nothing but reflect upon the abysmal level of self-absorption we have sunk to.

I was raised in an era in which community orientation was the order of the day. The family down the street, up the street, and even around the corner, were known to me. Nowadays, we intentionally simply do not even want to touch each other. Tragically, this societal malady has even spread to the church, which ought to be the bastion of hope for the sustenance of the legacy of love that Christ Jesus bequeathed to His family at Ascension. The current trend of what we call the "mega church" has birthed ministries in which the majority of the congregation have little or no contact with each other, from one week to the next, which also explains why we are making little or no impact on the society we are supposed to be serving and nurturing with the Good News of Christ. The Bible reveals that Jesus could have thousands thronging Him and He still had time for just one person, if that was what it took. In John chapter 5, Jesus encounters a man at the Pool of Bethesda where there was a host of sick people. Yet, He only had dialogue with one man who had been sick for thirty eight years. An angel came to "stir up" the water at a certain time of the year and whoever stepped into the pool was made well. To the naked eye it would appear to be heartless that only this one man experienced the healing power of Jesus on that day. In truth, however, that one man was His assignment on that day, and at that pond.

I am reminded of my attendance, some years ago, at what was supposed to be a tent revival, in Baltimore, Maryland. Upon arrival, nothing was in place to even remotely suggest the imminence of the event. I was installed in a room pending when arrangements would have been concluded. At the end of a three-hour wait, nothing was still in place. I informed the organizers that I could wait no longer as I had two services to conduct the next morning at our church.AsI was leaving the building, a young pregnant lady came in. Greeting her, I asked when she was due. She replied that her expected date of delivery was in about a month. However, the doctors were concerned because the baby was in the breech position. I asked if I could pray for her. As I prayed, I could feel the baby turning in her womb.

When I reached my car, the Holy Spirit revealed to me that I was not sent there for a tent revival, but had to wait the entire three hours until the woman showed up. If I had allowed my emotions get the better of me, and left earlier in a huff, I would not have fulfilled my assignment for that day. *"Then Jesus went about all the cities and villages, teaching in their synagogues, preaching the gospel of the Kingdom, and healing every sickness and every disease among the people. But when He saw the multitudes, He was moved with compassion for them, because they were weary and scattered, like sheep having no shepherd." (Mt 9: 35-36).* Imagine the collective sense of belonging that had to be generated in the hearts and minds of the people. We must not forget that they were under the oppressive rule of Rome at that time, and were fervently longing for the arrival of the prophesied Messiah. Unfortunately, however, many of the Jews did not believe that Jesus was the Messiah, and even to this present day there are still many of them that believe He was not the awaited Messiah. It is estimated that only 1.9% of the population of Israel is Christian. That is nothing short of an alarming statistic when we contemplate that this is the birth place of Christ.

The canonical record is clear that everywhere Jesus went, His mission was to relieve human suffering wherever He found it. *"And He came down with them and stood on a level place with a crowd of His disciples and a great multitude of people from all Judea and Jerusalem, and from the seacoast of Tyre and Sidon, who came to hear Him and be healed of their diseases, as well as those who were tormented with unclean spirits. And they were healed. And the whole multitude sought to touch Him, for power went out from Him and healed them all." (Lk 6: 17-19).* In other words He made time for everyone. As I stated earlier in this chapter, Jesus displayed the full range of the human emotions. He even cried. For many men, this is a very sensitive subject of discourse, primarily because many men are taught as young boys that a *real* man simply does not cry. As far as some men are concerned, only weak men cry. Yet, Jesus cried on more than one occasion. Permit me to say this parenthetically. Research findings document the scientific fact that when we don't allow ourselves to experience those emotions that come from the heart, we could end up with physical illness. That is because the body needs a release valve for pent up emotions. When this release valve is blocked, it could very well result in physical ailment. For most women, the expression of emotion comes with infinite ease, while men stifle theirs, and end up suffering heart attacks, strokes, and ulcers. There is absolutely nothing wrong with crying, for if there was, our heavenly Father would have never bothered to equip us with the emotions of despair, sadness and joy that seek expression through tears. In fact, it is also biblically a treasure to God. *"You number my wanderings; put my tears into Your bottle; are they not in Your book?" (Ps 56:8).* This should be reason enough for every believer to rejoice, knowing that our heavenly Father stores our tears in His bottle.

Empathy appears to be an emotion that few possess. Having *empathy* means that we allow ourselves to feel what others are going through. The news on the world's popular cable networks are a daily study in human tragedy; from shootings to domestic fires, and from wild fires to natural catastrophes. I have personally known people who have lost everything materially and had to start all over again. Having that type of experience ought to always make us empathetic toward someone else, and what they might be going through. That was definitely the sort of heart that Jesus possessed. *"Now as He drew near, He saw the city and wept over it." (Lk 19: 41).* What is it about us that has made our hearts so cold and callous toward our fellow man? Simply because that adverse incident is not happening to you at this moment in time does not quite mean you are entirely immune to its occurrence in your own life. On the other side of the coin, Jesus also displayed anger, but never to the degree that He lost control of Himself. For the most part His anger was displayed merely to express righteous indignation. *"Now the Passover of the Jews was at hand, and Jesus went up to Jerusalem. And He found in the temple those who sold oxen and sheep and doves, and the money changers doing business. When He had made a whip of cords, He drove them all out of the temple, with the sheep and oxen, and poured out the money changers' money and overturned the tables. And He said to those who sold doves; Take these things away! Do not make My Father's house a house of merchandise!" (Jn 2:13-16).* Mark also adds, *"And He would not allow anyone to carry wares through the temple. Then He taught, saying to them,*

CHAPTER SEVEN: Jesus Led With Emotional Intelligence

Is it not written, My house shall be called a house of prayer for all nations? But you have made it a den of thieves." (Mk 11:16-17). Even though Jesus was incensed at what they were doing in the temple, He yet remained completely under control throughout the entire episode. He released His anger with and for a definite purpose. Whenever I read that passage, I often wonder what would have transpired if Jesus had fully lost His temper on that day. I am of the absolute conviction that someone may have died.

Jesus provides the perfect template for ultimate leadership. One might be forgiven for thinking this would be the perfect leadership lesson for a "hothead"like Peter. Were Peter to have been in Jesus' shoes in the temple, on that day of unholy merchandising, someone might quite easily have lost a limb. All of us, and not just the contemporary leaders of today, ought to be inspired by the outstanding example that Jesus sets before us as the standard for emotional intelligence. An inalienable component of emotional intelligence is self-awareness, absence of which can lead to self-destruction. If we are not careful, we can so easily cultivate an indifferent disposition toward others that we blissfully believe that it is never our fault but everyone else's. At the other end of the spectrum, there are some people who are prone to states of melancholy. It is almost as if they live with a cloud constantly hanging over their head, and can never explain to anyone why that is so. Such individuals are definitely not in control of their emotions.

Further evaluation of, especially people who are so melancholic that they isolate themselves, often reveals that their thinking is adversely affected. Such thought processes will obviously result in emotions that will not be in alignment with God's will or His word. Worse, because of that parlous emotional state, one might not even care a single bit that one's thoughts are not in alignment with God's will. This is why a believer must be ruled by the peace of God. *"And let the peace of God rule in your hearts, to which also you were called in one body, and be thankful."* (Col 3:15). The Greek word for "rule," *Brabeuo,* which in ancient times was used to describethe umpireorrefereewho moderated and judged the athletic competitions that were so popular in the ancient world. Paul uses this word to tell us that the peace of God can work like an umpire or referee in our hearts, minds, and emotions. When detrimental emotions attempt to exert control over us or try to throw us into an emotional frenzy, we can stop it from happening by making the choice to let God's peace rise up from deep inside us like an umpire or referee to moderate our emotions. As we do so, we will be kept under the control of that divine peace as it rules in our hearts. When this divine umpire called *"peace"* steps into the game, it suddenly begins to call the shots and make all the decisions instead of our anxiety and worry.

Take our commonplace baseball, for instance. The umpire stands behind the plate and pronounces whether a pitch is a ball or a strike. We can draw a corollary from this. We should allow the *"spirit of peace"* to call the *balls and strikes* in our life. When our emotions are not under leash, we will think everything is a strike that demands our attention, when in actuality it is out of the strike zone. Here, once again, we can draw on the mastery of Jesus, and how He was always composed, and never allowed sensitive situations or indifferent people to *"push His buttons"* and cause Him to act out of character. I invite you to ponder for just a moment how you might react if someone spat on your face. I wouldn't be exaggerating if I said such a person should be prepared for the *"mother of all fights."* The act of spitting on someone is not considered merely despicable and utterly humiliating, but also the ultimate, and unmitigated insult. Let us critically examine how Jesus handled insult. *"He was oppressed and He was afflicted, yet, He opened not His mouth; He was led as a lamb to the slaughter, and as a sheep before its shearers is silent, so He opened not His mouth." (Isa 53: 7).* I consider myself someone who has achieved a certain level of spiritual maturity. Yet, I'm not entirely certain I could have handled the situation in that manner. One can only imagine the level of spiritual strength, faith, and courage it took to withstand the level of brutality that Jesus endured.

Today's average believer does not have to endure that type of wickedness, except perhaps in some third world countries where what is considered heretical to the religious order of that country is met with certain death. This chapter cannot end without addressing the truth that our emotions share the same groove with our attitude. Therefore, love must be the centerpiece of every Christian life. The spirit of love will void, negate, and eliminate any sort of negative emotions that are not a reflection of the *Christ Attitude*. *"And those who are Christ's have crucified the flesh with its passions and desires." (Gal 5: 24).* As an ambassador of the Kingdom of God, just one vile display of rash behavior would be enough to destroy any hope of winning someone who was leaning toward surrendering his or her life to Christ. Christ must be Lord of all or He is not Lord at all. It is that simple.

Prayer of Focus

Lord, make me an oasis of peace,
Such that I might visit hatred with a charitable heart;
Such that I might visit offense with forgiveness;
Such that I might visit chaos with order;
Such that I might visit discord with harmony;
Such that I might visit anxiety with an offer of faith;
Such that I might visit despair with renewed hope;
Such that I might visit agony with compassion;
Lord, grant me access to your divine presence;
That I might be an oasis of peace for all mankind.
In Jesus Name. Amen.

CHAPTER EIGHT

Jesus Led With Courage

"................Take courage! It is I. Don't be afraid."
(Matt 14:27 NIV)

I grew up in what, in America, is called the *inner city*. The term *inner city* is used as a euphemism for majority-minority lower-income residential districts that often refer to rundown neighborhoods, in a downtown or city center area. In a nutshell, the inner city is a distressed urban and suburban area of acknowledged poverty and low income. In the United States, inner city residents represent fully 14% of the population, which is about 45 million people. It goes without saying that life and living in such neighborhoods come with their own peculiar challenges. Growing up in the inner city demanded that one know how to "handle" oneself. In stark terms, that simply means there are those hair raising times when you just had to know how to defend yourself, or you might end up the hapless target of just about any and every bully in the neighborhood.

My case was all the more unfortunate because, having accepted Christ from an uncommonly tender age, I was your quintessential "church boy." Yet, despite being branded a church boy, it still became a matter of inevitability that I would find myself in the middle of a few of the sort of skirmishes that one might expect in such a neighborhood as ours. There was a paradox to it. My father and mother were the last parents that would ever advocate violence as a means of settling disputes of any kind. But, they were emphatic on the need, if not even the compelling necessity, that we just had to learn how to protect ourselves. Indeed, a couple of times I even found myself engaging in fisticuffs on behalf of my siblings because I was the oldest. I, more or less, learned courage through default. You either fought, or you found yourself the brunt of relentless and never-abating vicious taunts from others.

When I arrived at an understanding of what it meant to have Christ in my life, I also discovered that being courageous had another dimension to it. Undoubtedly, the enemy of our soul considers himself the ultimate bully, and if we are not strong in faith, we can easily become a perpetual target for his attacks. *"Be sober, be vigilant, because your adversary the devil walks about like a roaring lion, seeking whom he may devour."* (1 Pet 5: 8). It is in the matter of courage that Jesus, again, masterfully demonstrates with His disciples how we ought to carry ourselves in a world that appears malevolently designed to distract us from a path of *peaceful* and *peaceable* living. Instructively, there was never a time when we saw Jesus intimidated or threatened by the ravings of the religious order of the day. The irony was that it was those who loudly proclaimed themselves to be the last word in *piety* that were, in the same instance, apart from being a thorn in His flesh by being his primary traducers and *agent provocateurs,* also the primary source of contention He had to deal with, in courage, and in wisdom.

Any believer who is a true student of the Bible will only be too aware of the fact that it was the same people who loudly professed to an uncommonly holy relationship with God that, in eventually also turning out to be the most misguided in the population, were ultimately responsible for the

CHAPTER EIGHT: Jesus Led With Courage

crucifixion of Jesus. Even though the Messiah had long been prophesied to come, they were not prepared to receive Him because he didn't make His auspicious appearance riding on a white charger, and escorted by a retinue of attendants and hangers-on. No protocol attended His appearance. The usual, elaborate display of pomp and pageantry that attends the grandeur of eminence was absent in a man who gradually grew into the consciousness of the people as the messiah, rather one who made a sudden, Earth-shaking entry into the world as its savior. Humankind has always been steeped in, and will remain fixated on, its expectations of imperial grandeur from its leaders. It never occurred to anyone that the Son of Man would come as meek as a lamb.

"Rejoice greatly, O daughter of Zion! Shout, O daughter of Jerusalem! Behold, your King is coming to you; He is just and having salvation, lowly and riding on a donkey, a colt, the foal of a donkey." (Zech 9: 9). Ordinarily, one might have thought it near-inconceivable that there would be any doubt whatsoever that Jesus was indeed the Messiah. As it were, the prophets were simply not to be believed by a skeptical population. Primarily, the Master stood all alone to face and withstand tremendous opposition because the disciples were of little help in most of such situations. We must bear in mind that the disciples were no more than apprentices. They were learners who were unable to provide any type of security for Jesus. Scripture reveals that at least one of them, if not more, at one point, was prepared to die in the stead of Jesus when His life was threatened in Jerusalem. I have had cause to marvel that they could entertain even minimal dismay of any kind after witnessing the miracles, signs and wonders that they were privy to with the Master on a daily basis.

To render matters even more awe-inspiring, Jesus never backed down from any confrontation, especially from those that went as far as to cast doubts on His origin *"When He had come to His own country, He taught them in their synagogue, so that they were astonished and said: Where did this Man get this wisdom and these mighty works? Is this not the carpenter's son? Is not His mother called Mary? And His brothers James, Joses, Simon, and Judas? And His sisters, are they not all with us? Where then did this Man get all these things?" (Mt 13: 54-56).* The primary source of their astonishment was the fact that, based on his family tree, it was simply inconceivable for Him to be in possession of this awesome power. No one in His family had ever demonstrated such possibilities, talk less of such capabilities, and so there was no absolutely way what they were seeing could be legitimate. Indeed, there must have been times when He would have felt a despairing sense of frustration with such pronouncements from people He had been sent to salvage from sin, but certainly not to the degree that He ever sought to retaliate in any manner. Whenever a person is confident in who they are, and what their purpose is, such a person can remain secure in their sense of mission, and with a certain incontestable bravado. Besides that, Jesus was in full assurance that He had the full support of His heavenly Father at all times. Peter, who was often the spokesperson for the disciples, thought that he could fill the role of the Lord's "bodyguard," but Jesusmade it abundantly clear that his protection was not necessary. From that time, Jesus also began to make it clear to His disciples that He must go to Jerusalem, and suffer many things from the elders and chief priests and scribes, and be killed, and be raised on the third day. *"Then Peter took Him aside and began to rebuke Him, saying, Far be it from You, Lord, this shall not happen to You! But He turned and said to Peter; Get behind Me, Satan! You are an offense to Me, for you are not mindful of the things of God, but the things of men." (Mt 16: 21-23).* It is very humbling when we think that this Man was willing to take on the sin of the entire world without fear. Although He had a human moment, He still faced death; the most inhumane death a man could experience in that era, yet

CHAPTER EIGHT: Jesus Led With Courage

He faced it with uncommon courage.

Jesus sets the standard for all of us, His brothers and sisters, as to how we are to approach the trials of life; be they emotional, physical, financial, marital, or spiritual. Our response to life is going to be predicated upon our perspective. The best perspective to adopt is that we do not have a problem. Rather, we merely have lessons to learn from a challenge. *"Who, in the days of His flesh, when He had offered up prayers and supplications, with vehement cries and tears to Him who was able to save Him from death, and was heard because of His godly fear, though He was a Son, yet He learned obedience by the things which He suffered." (Heb 5: 7-8).* I also believe that our confidence will soar when we understand that we don't *come* from God, but that we are *sent* by God. There is a specific problem in the Earthly realm that each of us has been specifically sent to address. The generality are frustrated to no end because they haven't quite discovered what they were sent to accomplish here on Earth. *If one hasn't the slightest clue as to one's mission on Earth, how can one approach life with courage?*

Nothing is quite so easy to mistake for a mean-spirited attitude as courage. Behind that veneer of cynicism is a person who is afflicted with no little inner turmoil, and who would have others believe that they have no fear. In real and stark terms, the world is actually in total ignorance of the *authentic self* of such a person. Imagine the myriad of unsavory situations that people find themselves in that might well have been averted if only people had been in the proper place at the right time. An outstanding quality that Jesus possessed was *discernment.* More often than not, He knew the thoughts of others, and was not averse to speaking the *truth* into any issue that called for *truth.* Let us, for a moment, imagine just how charged the atmosphere might have been during some of those confrontations. *"So the scribes and Pharisees watched Him closely, whether He would heal on the Sabbath, that they might find an accusation against Him. But He knew their thoughts, and said to the man who had the withered hand; Arise and stand here! And he arose and stood. Then Jesus said to them: I will ask you one thing; is it lawful on the Sabbath to do good or to do evil, to save life or to destroy? And when He had looked around at them all, He said to the man; Stretch out your hand. And he did so, and his hand was restored as whole as the other. But they were filled with rage, and discussed with one another what they might do to Jesus." (Lk 6:6-11).* Imagine what our world would be like if all of the present day citizens of the Kingdom possessed the same spirit!

Even though during Jesus' tenure here on Earth, the disciples were very passive, after His ascent to heaven they became much more courageous. Peter, who at one point was rather quite boisterous, but never really lived up to much of what he claimed he would or could do, eventually made a hundred and eighty degree turnaround. We know he swung a sword in the Garden of Gethsemane, only for him to ultimately turn round and flee like the rest of the disciples. The sort of radical change necessary to correct the terrible ills bedeviling our society today will never come to pass as long as the Body of Christ chooses to remain quiet, and in the background, in the face of blatant travesty of the truth, and the praiseworthy. Scripture reveals that many of the New Testament saints were willing to put their life on the line for the cause of Christ. It is tragic that, in the world of today, such fervor, and such willingness to die for a cause, totally misguided as it is, is true only of the religions that don't embrace Christ. The adherents of those religions are willing to blow up airplanes, destroy massive buildings, and even strap a bomb to themselves, for what they believe in. I hasten to repeat that this is by no means an endorsement of their acts, and merely wish to express that such fervor is what Christendom needs in these dire times of ignominy amongst the Body of

CHAPTER EIGHT: Jesus Led With Courage

Christ. *"Now, Lord, look on their threats, and grant to your servants that with all boldness they may speak Your word, by stretching out Your hand to heal, and that signs and wonders may be done through the name of Your holy Servant Jesus. And when they had prayed, the place where they were assembled together was shaken, and they were all filled with the Holy Spirit, and they spoke the word of God with boldness." (Acts 4: 29-31).* It would be tragically remiss of me, if in this treatise I failed to mention some of the people who, in recent memory, have taken a firm stance in support of the Kingdom at the risk of their freedom and financial stability. Kim Davis, the former clerk at Rowan County, Kentucky, was incarcerated for refusing to issue marriage licenses to homosexual couples. Jack Phillips, a baker in Colorado was sued by a homosexual couple for not making a cake for a homosexual wedding, although he gained a partial victory at the Supreme Court for the protection of his rights, only to have another person recently sue him because he refused to make a "gender transition" cake. Apparently, the enemy of our soul is not going to rest until we are completely silenced in the world. *"Let the redeemed of the Lord say so, whom He has redeemed from the hand of the enemy." (Ps 107: 2).*

Courage is not the absence of fear. Courage is the mastery of fear. It is true. Courage does not connote a total absence of fear. The total absence of fear would be nothing short of an adventure in fatalism, as fear defines the boundaries of mortal adventure, effectively curtailing our all-too-human propensity to willfully and blithely glide into misadventure. We are reminded of the time Jesus repaired, all alone, to the mountainside to pray, and to meditate. Shortly before dawn, bringing His solitude to a satisfactory conclusion, He came down from the mountain, by which time the boat, driven by the strong, tidal waves, had sailed a considerable distance from land. Without much ado, the Master stepped onto the water, and started walking on the lake towards the boat. When His disciples saw a man walking on the lake, they thought they were seeing an apparition, and became absolutely terrified.

"Take courage! It is me. Do not be afraid," Jesus called out, from the distance.

"Lord, if it is truly you, tell me to come to you on the water," Peter replied.

"come!" Jesus replied simply.

Confidently, Peter climbed out of the boat, and walked on the water towards Him. However, the gusts of ocean wind suddenly became even more ferocious. In his terror, Peter took his eyes off Him, even as his courage failed him. As the waves swirled violently around him, he began to sink.

"Lord, save me!" Peter cried out.

Instantly, He reached out his hand and caught Peter, saying, *"You of little faith, why did you doubt?"*

Just as peter sank because of his fear, that is how many have sunk, and are still sinking, in their spiritual, business and professional lives. Fear is the most potent enemy of human accomplishment. It can easily subsume or bury one's purpose. It is fear that buries the purpose, passion and gifts of many people, preventing them from achieving their true life potential. *Our greatest challenge is the conquest of fear and the development of courage, and since anything we practice over and again eventually becomes a habit, we can only develop the habit of courage by acting courageously anytime courage is called for.* Courage, which is a result of confident faith, is not the absence of fear. Rather, it is the mastery of fear. A courageous person goes forward in spite of his fear. Anytime we find our faith failing us, we need look no further than the words in Isaiah 41:10, *"So do not fear, for I am with you, do not be dismayed, for I am your God. I will strengthen you and help you; I will uphold you*

CHAPTER EIGHT: Jesus Led With Courage

with my righteous right hand."

Time and again, Jesus modeled the courage He was desirous of teaching His disciples. One can only imagine the sort of intestinal fortitude it took for Him not to respond to, or retaliate against, the unspeakable humiliation of the Roman soldiers who beat Him mercilessly, spit on Him, and disparaged Him with all manner of verbal onslaught. On a personally truthful note, I don't know if I could have handled all that without itching to fight back in some way. However, He set the standard so well that a young disciple named Stephen was able to take a stand, and be brutally stoned to death. Even while being stoned, Stephen still had the graciousness to pray for forgiveness for his attackers. *"When they heard these things they were cut to the heart, and they gnashed at him with their teeth. But he, being full of the Holy Spirit, gazed into heaven and saw the glory of God and Jesus standing at the right hand of God, and said, Look I see the heavens opened and the Son of man standing at the right hand of God! Then they cried out with a loud voice, stopped their ears, and ran at him with one accord, and they cast him out of the city and stoned him. And the witnesses laid down their clothes at the feet of a young man named Saul. And they stoned Stephen as he was calling on God and saying, Lord Jesus, receive my spirit. Then he knelt down and cried out with a loud voice, Lord, do not charge them with this sin. And when he had said this, he fell asleep."* *(Acts 7: 54-60)*. At no more auspicious time in the annals of Christendom is it imperative for Kingdom citizens to stand up for what they believe in.

Without doubt, this will vary from one person to another, largely because of our varying backgrounds and differing belief systems, but I often wonder why is it that when the Bible is so very clear on how we are supposed to be of one heart and one mind, it has proved one of the greatest challenges amongst the Body of Christ. *"Therefore if there is any consolation in Christ, if any comfort of love, if any fellowship of the Spirit, if any affection and mercy, fulfill my joy by being like-minded, having the same love, being of one accord, of one mind. Let nothing be done through selfish ambition or conceit, but in lowliness of mind let each esteem others better than himself. Let each of you look out not only for his own interests, but also for the interests of others. Let this mind be in you which was also in Christ Jesus, who, being in the form of God, did not consider it robbery to be equal with God, but made Himself of no reputation, taking the form of a bondservant, and coming in the likeness of men." (Phil 2:1-7).* Expectedly, the generality will consider this divine prescription a rather tall ambition, if not even utterly impossible. I beg to differ. Whenever I watch a sporting event, particularly football, I can't help but notice the solidarity people display in the unalloyed support of their own chosen team. As the cameras pan a stadium of 50,000 or more, we notice that almost everyone has religiously adorned their team's colors. Others come in all manner of outrageous costume, perfectly willing to make themselves look as ridiculous as possible, just so as to revel in the team spirit of the moment. At such times of sporting hilarity, the question always looms large in my mind, *"Why doesn't this happen in the Body of Christ?"* God says our love should be unconditional, and it does appear as if the world gets it, at least for three or four hours every Sunday. I will never forget a statement I heard while watching the movie, *Concussion*. Will Smith played the role of a coroner of some notable reputation. He had noticed something that appeared to be a common denominator in some deceased football players, and he embarked on an in-depth research. His boss told him that he was about to stir up the hornet's nest, *"...........because you are about to take on the NFL, and the NFL is now the owner of a day that used to belong to the church!"*

The movie ended right there for me. I simply could not get

past that statement. That statement implied, with barely concealed cynicism, that football had become many people's god. That was also a crystal clear indictment of the church, since it also made clear that we were asleep at the wheel as the enemy hijacked a day of worship from us. There is no gainsaying the fact many a man in the fold of so-called believers would gleefully dispense with church worship if its hours as much as coincided with that of a football game. I have a sneaky suspicion that this was strategically done, and when you add the Covid-19 pandemic to the picture, more and more people have reason not to come to worship because it is an inconvenience. Not enough pastors have had the courage to boldly speak about this erosion in the value we used to attach to worship, leading to the closure of many of our houses of worship. Multitudes are dying without Christ, yet the church is supposed to be the medium for the world to learn about Him. *"His intent was that now, through the church, the manifold wisdom of God should be made known to the rulers and authorities in the heavenly realms, according to his eternal purpose that he accomplished in Christ Jesus our Lord. In him and through faith in him we may approach God with freedom and confidence." (Eph 3: 10-12 (NIV).* This, undoubtedly, requires courage. Yet, we must never forget that courage is not the absence of fear, but rather, the ability to act in spite of fear. There will always be people that demonstrate courage. It is not that such people were not afraid. They were merely willing, despite their fear, to take the risk. That takes courage. Courage will cause us to go to greater lengths than we ever have before, and that contributes to our growth. Ultimately, to live courageously is going to require a confrontation with *ourself*. Choosing that which is comfortable or convenient may be easy, but to go to the next dimension means to abandon the old ways and mundane ways of thinking. Let us follow the *Leader*. Let us follow Jesus.

Prayer of Focus

Lord, You have told me in your Word to "be strong and of a good courage" and to "fear not," and I need your help to do that. You have said that "I can do all things through Christ which strengtheneth me." Please help me be strong and courageous today and walk in your strength. I know I can do nothing on my own. I am weak and powerless without You. I know it is only through You and your strength that I can face the giants in my way. Just as David prayed to You and proclaimed, "The Lord is my shepherd, I shall not want." "Yea, though I walk through the valley of the shadow of death, I will fear no evil: for thou art with me; thy rod and thy staff they comfort me." Lord help me to be like David and trust in you, lead me beside your still waters, restore my soul, and give me the courage and strength this day to do your will. Amen. In Jesus' name. Amen.

CHAPTER NINE

Jesus Led With Gratitude

"And Jesus lifted up His eyes and said: Father, I thank You that You have heard Me. And I know that You always hear Me, but because of the people who are standing by I said this, that they may believe that You sent Me." (Jn 11 : 41-42)

Absolutely nothing can become quite as easy for us, as observers of Jesus, through scripture, to see Him only through the lens of miracles, signs, and wonders. In stretching the boundaries of the logic of His incontrovertible divinity even further, one might even be forgiven for easily concluding that there ought not to be the faintest need for Him to express gratitude for anything especially since, in any case, He is not only the Son of God, but also God in the flesh. Yet, as I have candidly expressed in preceding chapters, it would merely serve to defy God's own intention for the mission of Christ on Earth to be sanctimoniously dismissive of the humanity of Christ. Expressed quite simply, that humanity serves the divine purpose of establishing an interface that is both a common denominator, and one of genuine utility, between Jesus and Man. No passage provides effortless corroboration of that truth than, *"And Jesus lifted up His eyes and said: Father, I thank You that You have heard Me. And I know that You always hear Me, but because of the people who are standing by I said this, that they may believe that You sent Me." (Jn 11 : 41-42).*

The lesson here is as simple as it is clear. There ought to never be a time in our journey as believers that we become so supercilious as to assume that we have somehow made such sufficiently total provision for ourselves that we need not express our heartfelt and sincere gratitude to Almighty God for His wonderful, benevolent and consistent provision for our needs on every conceivable level. The word of God is clear to the indisputable point of finality. He is the reason why we live, and move, and have our very being. Additionally, it behoves us to never forget the numerous times in which we were delivered from situations that very well could have been demoralizing, if not even catastrophic. The Book of Psalms is replete with the bottomless expression of thanksgiving by King David, who on more than one occasion committed sins that were nothing short of a terrible affront to God. Yet, in each instance, he turned to God in a spirit of repentance, and thanked Him for sparing his life, and never abandoning him. *"Hide Your face from my sins, and blot out all my iniquities, create in me a clean heart, O God, and renew a steadfast spirit within me, do not cast me away from Your presence, and do not take Your Holy Spirit from me. Restore to me the joy of Your salvation and uphold me by Your generous Spirit." (Ps 51: 9-12).*

Empirical evidence abounds that Jesus had, and demonstrated, the utmost respect for His heavenly Father. Obedient to the Father in every conceivable way, He never, not at anytime, in His life and ministry, displayed anything that even remotely resembled a self-important attitude to His Father. He constantly lived with a spirit of humility, surprisingly not only in His relationship with His Father, but also with all who encountered Him in the course of His Earthly work, including His Earthly parents, disciples, and even His traducers. No wonder the Apostle Paul admonished us that

CHAPTER NINE: Jesus Led With Gratitude

we should emulate the mindset of Jesus in our daily lives. *"Let this mind be in you which was also in Christ Jesus, who, being in the form of God, did not consider it robbery to be equal with God, but made Himself of no reputation, taking the form of a bondservant, and coming in the likeness of men, and being found in appearance as a man, He humbled Himself and became obedient to the point of death, even the death of the cross." (Phil 2: 5-8).* Any attempt at fully understanding this in totality can only be an exercise in futility, and this assertion is most certainly so, unless we are able to comprehend what even the Old Testament says about us. *"I said; You are gods, and all of you are children of the Most High!" (Ps 82: 6).* This is repeated in Jn 10: 34. *"Jesus answered them, "Is it not written in your law, 'I said, "You are gods?"* I am only too aware that this type of statement is such a radical departure from what even the most discerning amongst us can grasp, even in its simplest connotation, and that explains why it is so difficult for many of us to handle it. Nonetheless, is eminently true of us. Could it be that this is a large part of the reason why so many of God's people live far beneath their divinely-ordained privilege? My pertinent assertions, in due regard, are not made to foster, or to generate thoughts that are not in alignment with the word of God. Rather, they are deliberately contrived to prayerfully elevate the thinking of many that are seemingly incapacitated by an inability to accept their God-given status.

It is my fervent hope that our lofty God-endowed status ought to, at the very least, provoke and elicit an even greater sense of gratitude from each one of us as we embrace just who we are in Christ Jesus. Let us remain in keen awareness of the fact that Jesus never took, nor even accepted credit for anything He did. *"Then Jesus answered and said to them; Most assuredly I say to you, the Son can do nothing of Himself, but what He sees the Father do; for whatever He does, the Son also does in like manner." (Jn 5: 19).* These words of Jesus are in total alignment with what He said in Jn 14: 12. *"Most assuredly, I say to you, he who believes in Me, the works that I do he will do also; and greater works than these he will do, because I go to My Father."* With those eternally relevant words, He assured us that we *can* do the things we observe Him doing, and greater works, if we believe. A particular in that statement speaks eloquently what stands between us and untold miracles. That word is *believe*. We are afflicted with *unbelief.* Nothing is more perplexing as the strange fact that the Body of Christ struggles, at best, at fulfilling the will of God on Earth. One can't help wondering if that is not unfortunately so for the rather prosaic reason that most of us labor under the grand illusion that the Lord will accomplish great things in our lives without even minimal effort on our part. This assumption is as false as it gravely indicts us for our insufferable sense of self-entitlement. What we so abysmally fail to understand is that we are co-laborers with Christ; a fact that Jesus was fully acquainted with. On my own part, I am often bewildered anytime I contemplate how amazing it is that the God of the entire universe would want to use me to work in collaboration with Him to salvage all of mankind.

That notion, all on its own, ought to provoke thoughts of gratitude and thankfulness, especially when we think of the impact we can be privileged to have on the life and destiny trajectory of the people of this planet called Earth. First and foremost, one should never lose sight of the example that the Lord Jesus Christ presents to us to follow. No wonder the Father loved Him so much. Pause for a moment to imagine how Jesus lived such a spotless and unblemished life, yet remained in unflinching submission to His heavenly Father at all times. I am of the conviction that American citizenship has undoubtedly spoiled the best of us. It would seem that being citizens of a nation where abundance abounds, we have become the spoiled and privileged brats of an indulgent society. We have collectively graduated to the point where we take virtually everything for granted, and in the process, it would appear that many of us even actually believe that God, somehow, owes us a favor. The truth, however, is more earth-shaking than that. While we most certainly do not have to earn the Lord's love, we also simply cannot continue to blissfully wallow in the insufferably arrogant and presumptuous notion that the Lord is some sort of cosmic genie, and all we need do is rub the Bible, and untold blessings will come pouring out of that holy book. What the Body of Christ does not seem to realize is that it has a sober spiritual assignment, and that obligation is to conscientiously reflect the image of Christ on Earth. We are to represent Christ alive in us, as we are living, and going through life in the world. That is what is meant by *"your body is the temple of God."* He lives is us; and He wants to radiate out of us in our words, attitude, and actions. God wants to empower us as we talk, as we live, as we think, and as we act. God wants to flow out of us, and into our *sin-sickened* and *sin-darkened* world. In other words, we are supposed to *live like Christ in a Christ-less world.* What is more, we were saved to spend the rest of our lives being the only reflection of Christ most people will ever get to see. That is right. *We are the only true reflection of Christ most people will ever get to see.* In fact, thereare people in our life for whom we will become the closest thing to Jesus Christ they will ever see. We are tasked by God to live a Christ-reflecting life, no matter what the world, our society, or the cultural norms around us may dictate. That call to reflect God in our lives has always been the same for every believer from the Garden of Eden onward. After all, Joseph reflected God in his life when he was in Egypt. "And Pharaoh said to his servants, *"Can we find such a oneas this, a man in whom is the Spirit of God?" (Gen 41:38).* Daniel, too, reflected God in his life when he was in Babylon. *"I have heard of you, that the Spirit of God isin you, and thatlight and understanding and excellent wisdom are found in you." (Dan 5:14)*. If Christ is not seen in our life, and by people around us, it is because we don't want Him to be seen in us, and not because God is unable to shine through us. We must *desire* to reflect Him. We must ask to be reflections of His grace and power. Perhaps that is what Paul meant by these words. *"Therefore, as the elect of God, holy and beloved, put on tender mercies, kindness, humility, meekness, longsuffering; bearing with one another, and forgiving one another, if anyone has a complaint against another; even as Christ forgave you, so you also must do. But above all these things put on love, which is the bond of perfection. And let the peace of God rule in your hearts, to which also you were called in one body; and be thankful. Let the word of Christ dwell in you richly in all wisdom, teaching and admonishing one another in psalms and hymns and spiritual songs, singing with grace in your hearts to the Lord. And whatever you do in word or deed, do all in the name of the Lord Jesus, giving thanks to God the Father through Him." (Col 3:12-17)*.

Ultimately, however, we must remain in a state of profound gratitude for all that the Lord has done for us. There is no doubt that the Gen Z and Millennial generations live with a sense of entitlement. However, I would venture to say that their mental disposition has come from observing the generations before them. All of the societal lines that we are familiar with have become despairingly blurred, and it is now extremely difficult to even discern where right and wrong begin and end. Even the Old Testament prophets warned us that these days were going to come, yet we did not take heed. As I have previously stated, Jesus came to straighten out everything that was crooked. He desperately attempted to demonstrate to us just how intimate the Father wanted to be with us, but even His own family did not believe in Him. I am of a certainty that many a reader of this book will be able to bear witness with the Master as to how you also have been

CHAPTER NINE: Jesus Led With Gratitude

ridiculed and persecuted by those closest to you, all because of the path you chose to tread that was a departure from the status quo.

In my years of growth, we began each meal by giving thanks to God for providing for us from His bounty. Today we are viewed as being religious fanatics because we would dare bless our food, especially in public. Everything we have comes from God and we must thank Him for being such a prolific provider. Thanksgiving can only come out of a heart of humility, and the Lord rewards the man or woman that maintains a grateful heart. *"By humility and the fear of the Lord are riches and honor and life." (Prov 22: 4)*. All one has to do is observe the outpouring of the Holy Spirit that was quite visible in the life of Jesus. Additionally, the Father, on more than one occasion, voiced His pleasure over having Jesus as His son. *"When all the people were baptized, it came to pass that Jesus also was baptized, and while He prayed, the heaven was opened. And the Holy Spirit descended in bodily form like a dove upon Him, and a voice came from heaven which said: You are My beloved Son; in You I am well pleased." (Lk 3: 21-22)*. It would behove all of us to live our lives in such a way as to be able to hear the Father make such a statement about us. At anytime, Jesus could have determined that He wanted to exalt Himself while here on Earth, but that was never the case. To do that would have disqualified Him from being the perfect sacrifice. Leaders, in particular, need to guard themselves in this area. It is quite easy to fall prey to the temptation of thinking and believing that *"I was able to do all of this in my own power."* The Lord cautioned Israel against the same temptation. As has been proven time and again in the affairs of Man, his elevation often becomes tempting. Yet, God is simply not looking for celebrities. He is looking for ambassadors. The difference between *celebrities* and *ambassadors* is purpose. Each of us must possess a grateful heart when we realize that the God of the entire universe would dare to empower us with gifts, and then release us to minister to a lost and dying world. Life itself would not be available to us if it were not for the grace and mercy of Almighty God. The man or woman that is a leader ought not to dare boast or brag about their accomplishments or achievements, as they would be laying a bad precedent with those coming after them.

It is no wonder that the multitudes wanted to be in the presence of Jesus, not just because of the great miracles He performed among them, but also because He was touchable. In today's post-modern church, it is near-impossible to get close to some ecclesiastical leaders because of the protocol that attends them. It is a far cry from the example that the Lord Jesus sets for us when, even after ministering to thousands, He would still have time for the least of them. Does this imply that there are some among us that are not really grateful to God, and that they literally take Him for granted? *"Therefore, since we are receiving a Kingdom which cannot be shaken, let us be thankful, and so worship God acceptably with reverence and awe, for our God is a consuming fire." (Heb 12: 28-29).* Apparently, there is no longer a healthy fear of God, and this seems to lead to an attitude of ingratitude. The younger generations are very much different from the generations before them. Parents have inadvertently contributed to their mindset since they, the parents, claim they would make life easier for their children, so that they wouldn't have to live the way they lived. If only they could see and experience, firsthand, the levels of poverty and despair that exist in many other countries, they would quickly alter their disposition to one of humility and gratitude. For most Americans, it is simply inconceivable that they would have to decide which children would be able to partake of what little they had for a particular meal. Yet, that is the stark reality of some of the countries I have been privileged to visit in the course of my work in Christian ministry.

CHAPTER NINE: Jesus Led With Gratitude

There once was a young man who was a part of the ministry I pastored for many years. This remarkable young man provided a demonstration that very few exemplified. He had been incarcerated for a number of years, and on his release from prison, simply entered into a rare state of gratitude for everything. For him, a trip to the local variety store became a place of worship. He bought a candy bar, and before he opened it, he prayed over it, and gave God thanks. Some might think that to be far fetched, however, he was *just* grateful for *everything*. *"Give thanks, for this is the will of God in Christ Jesus concerning you." (1 Thess 5: 18).* The first prayer of each and everyday should be, *"Lord, I thank You for another day!"* Jesus set the stage for us as the example for every facet of life. Therefore, we have no excuse for not living the way the Word of God dictates. We are commanded to follow His example. *"For to this you were called, because Christ also suffered for us, leaving us an example, that you should follow His steps." (1 Pet 2: 21).* In truth, we have so much to be thankful for, and it would take the rest of our life to thank the Father for all that He has done. Again, Jesus set the standard. Let us make sure that we continue to lift it high.

Prayer of Focus

Create in me a clean heart, O God, and renew a steadfast spirit within me. Permeate my spirit with that attitude of gratitude that will be an eloquent reflection of the Christ-like Man that you always intended me to be. Allow me to so live in Christ that I might be a guiding Light for those who are groping their way through the dark alleys of their life. Finally, set me up as a template for all that is noble and righteous in gratitude for all that You have done, and continue to do for me. In Jesus name. Amen.

CHAPTER TEN

Jesus Was A Servant Leader

"Shepherd the flock of God which is among you, serving as overseers, not by compulsion but willingly, not for dishonest gain but eagerly; nor as being lords over those entrusted to you, but being examples to the flock." (1 Pet 5: 2-3).

Leadership is a concept that has been at the foundation of every society and culture throughout history, and because of his very unique leadership style, Jesus stands head and shoulders above the many great leaders that have had a profound impact and influence on mankind. Without doubt, Jesus modeled a novel style of leadership that infuriated the religious leaders of the day, in particular because of his penchant for mingling with the people, and standing up for them. Bishop T D Jakes once said that the man or woman that desires to be a quality leader must smell like sheep. This is a superb theology of, in general, *spiritual leadership,* and in particular, *pastoral care.* The beauty of the analogy is that it presents a compelling, practical, and biblically rich case for ministry as defined by the metaphor of shepherding. The eloquent case it makes is that true spiritual leadership is not one of distant and detached boardroom-like direction. Rather, it is one of intimate involvement with the sheep. Because of this intimate involvement, authentic leaders, who are actually shepherds who are out in the pasture, end up smelling like sheep they pasture. This is the kind of leadership that will effectively lead the church into the morally-turbulent twenty-first century. That is not expecting too much, as it was same kind of leadership that led the church through the morally and politically chaotic first century. It was this sort of *shepherding*; this sort of leadership that Jesus used, and this is the kind of leadership that will take His church where He wants it to go.

Not unexpectedly, the term "shepherd" evokes warm images of love, care, and tenderness. It also describes a form of leadership that is protective to the point of peril. It is a dangerous, dirty, and smelly brand of leadership. Shepherding is something that every follower of Christ, *The Good Shepherd*, is called to become. This Good Shepherd brand of leader is the biblical leader that is ideal for the future needs of the Christian community. It is the sort of leadership in which the leader must show him or herself to be reachable and touchable. At the very core of Jesus' leadership was His desire to be a servant to all people. He made it very clear that that was His mantra. *"For even the Son of man did not come to be served, but to serve, and to give His life a ransom for many." (Mk 10: 45).* In much of what we see in today's world, be it secular or spiritual, leaders are the exact opposite. There is now a prevailing elitist attitude to leadership that leaves the world's people helplessly left to cater to the egotistical ways of the leaders. What we experience today is even a far cry from what the Bible says about the man, Moses.

"Now the man Moses was very humble, more than all men who were on the face of the earth." (Num 12:3). In order for an organization to be effective and efficient, walls of distinction must be destroyed between leaders and the led. While, understandably, there will be functional differences in the roles played by leaders and those who work with them, no one should fall into the terrible temptation of thinking

CHAPTER TEN: Jesus Was A Servant Leader

they can be lord and master over others. Our heavenly Father never intended for us to dominate each other. Our dominion was supposed to be over our environment. In other words, domination was designed to be over all that encompassed the Earth; animals and nature. It was the fall of man that brought about the change in thinking, particularly when Cain took issues with his brother Abel, and slew him. It was from that day that humanity became beset with relational difficulties. No matter how far up the ladder we climb, no one has the right to look down their nose at anyone else. At the end of the day, we are all but dust. From dust we came, and to dust we shall return.

"Shepherd the flock of God which is among you, serving as overseers, not by compulsion but willingly, not for dishonest gain but eagerly; nor as being lords over those entrusted to you, but being examples to the flock." (1 Pet 5: 2-3). Today's world is selfish, rather than selfless. We live in the era of the "selfie." Not only do we take *pictures* that are selfies, but we also project *attitudes* that are selfies. Majority of us are so self-absorbed that the whole world might as well be revolving around only us. As I stated in a previous chapter, we have all but lost the whole concept of community; one in which we place the needs of others above and ahead of of our own. In essence, we are now a world of *takers*, and not givers. *"I have shown you in every way, by laboring like this, that you must support the weak. And remember the words of the Lord Jesus, that He said, it is more blessed to give than to receive." (Acts 20: 35).* We have somehow managed to carve out one day of the year that is somewhat reflective of this passage of scripture. That day is Christmas. Yet, a question looms large in one's mind. Are we doing it because of a genuine desire to be a blessing, or is it because it has been a tradition for so long, and we decidedly do not want to be seen as that member of the tribe that is not adhering to the tradition? The statistics reveal that Christmas is a time of

the year where the greatest number of suicides occur. A lot of people, beleaguered with thoughts of their financial inability to purchase hordes of presents, now see themselves as being inferior to others. Sadly, we are creating an ideology that will ultimately become the philosophy of younger generations, and drive us farther and farther apart.

From the very beginning of Jesus's ministry He was always very secure in who He was, and it was to who He was that He invited others to come and join Him. One of the attributes of a servant leader is the ability to empower others to become the best version of themselves. *But who, indeed, is a servant leader?* Servant leadership is a unique approach to leadership in which the leader puts the needs of others before his own desires, and acts first, as a servant. Christians are called to follow Jesus' example and become servant leaders in our spheres of influence. We can become great leaders by showing compassion, empowering others, and creating a culture of respect and collaboration. Leading with love and humility for God's glory makes a positive difference. Unfortunately, many overlook this concept of leadership today; a day in which leadership equates with nothing but raw power and blatant, overpowering authority. However, we have Jesus Christ to thank for the demonstration of the ultimate example of true leadership. His life and teachings demonstrate how important it is to lead with love, compassion, and a servant's heart. With an increasing need for true servant leaders to guide the members of the Body of Christ, those called to leadership positions must look to God's word for guidance. The ultimate servant leader follows Jesus Christ's example. I invite you to join me to look at several examples of Christian leadership in the words and actions of Christ Jesus.

Jesus demonstrated servant leadership by washing His disciples' feet, a task that was typically the job of the lowest servant in a household. Even though Jesus was God in human form, He humbled Himself to serve His disciples. This act

CHAPTER TEN: Jesus Was A Servant Leader

of service showed His humility and love for His followers. *"If I then, your Lord and Teacher, have washed your feet, you also ought to wash one another's feet. For I have given you an example, that you should do as I have done to you."* (John 13:14-15). Jesus also taught about the importance of serving others. *"For even the Son of Man did not come to be served, but to serve, and to give His life a ransom for many."* (Mk 10:45). These words show that Jesus not only believed in servant leadership, but He practiced it Himself, and this is reiterated in Philippians 2:3-4, *"Do nothing out of selfish ambition or vain conceit. Rather, in humility value others above yourselves, not looking to your own interests but each of you to the interests of the others."* It is important to understand the common good of God's people. It means placing your desires second place to the interest of your people. Humility is a hallmark trait of Christian leadership.

Another way Jesus demonstrated servant leadership was through His compassion for others. He showed care and concern for those who sick, oppressed, or rejected by society. *"But when He saw the multitudes, He was moved with compassion for them, because they were weary and scattered, like sheep having no shepherd."* (Mt 9:36). It was this compassion that led Him to heal the sick, feed the hungry, and befriend the outcasts of society. As Christians, God calls us to follow Jesus' example and become servant leaders in our spheres of influence. Compassionate leadership is particularly critical in kingdom work. Showing compassion means being willing to listen, care for, and help those in need. For example, in Mt 25:35-36, Jesus said, *"For I was hungry, and you gave me something to eat, I was thirsty, and you gave me something to drink, I was a stranger, and you invited me in, I needed clothes, and you clothed me, I was sick, and you looked after me, I was in prison, and you came to visit me."* When we show kindness and compassion to hurting people, we serve them with love, just as Jesus did.

Another way we can become servant leaders is by empowering others. When we empower someone else, we encourage and support them to use their gifts and talents to make a positive difference in the world. As leaders, we should create opportunities for others to grow, learn, and succeed. However, we should also be willing to step back and allow others to take the lead when it is appropriate. This kind of discernment requires a certain level of humility but also creates a culture of collaboration and respect. Today's modern world demands leaders that come to their job with an attitude of humility. We need leaders who exemplify an attitude of Christian leadership by being humble and compassionate. By acknowledging and valuing the needs of others, and the value they bring, Christian leaders can better serve their followers and create a culture of respect and trust.

Jesus was able to see past where the people were to assist them to go where they needed to be. Being a successful fisherman was not all that He saw. Being a tax collector, or even a doctor, was not all that he saw. *"And Jesus, walking by the Sea of Galilee, saw two brothers, Simon called Peter, and Andrew his brother, casting a net into the sea; for they were fishermen. Then He said to them, Follow Me, and I will make you fishers of men."* (Mt 4: 18-19). A true servant leader never boasts about their abilities. At any time, Jesus could have resorted to boasted about all that He had done, but most of the time, He actually implored others to say nothing about what He had done for them. *"When Jesus departed from there, two blind men followed Him, crying out and saying; Son of David, have mercy on us! And when He had come into the house, the blind men came to Him. And Jesus said to them: Do you believe that I am able to do this? They said to Him; yes Lord. Then He touched their eyes, saying, according to your faith let it be to you. And their eyes were opened. And Jesus sternly warned them, saying, See that no one knows it! But when they had departed, they spread the news about Him in all that country." (Mt 9: 27-31).* I can't say I blame them. It would be hard put to imagine that you would have a miracle of that magnitude done for you, and all you can do is keep to yourself. That would be rather atypical of conventional human nature. Yet, the vital point here is that Jesus never sought glory for anything that He did, and that ought to be a rather noble precedent for all of us; especially for those in leadership. *"Let another man praise you, and not your own mouth; a stranger and not your own lips." (Prov 27: 2).* An individual that has been, or is a leader, should have a greater degree of understanding of what it means to be in the position of a follower. I don't believe that any leader can be very effective if he or she has never known what it is to be a follower.

A true servant leader is one that does their level best to assist others in discovering, and then developing gifts and abilities that are, at times, dormant inside the other person. Any great visionary realizes that there is no way gifts and abilities, and by extension, stellar accomplishments, will be made manifest without collaborative team effort. Assisting others becomes an investment of sorts when someone within the ranks is given an opportunity to "shine." Remarkably, that human exaltation in achievement and esteem becomes a win for all involved. Nothing is lost to the leader when such victory is shared. Remember the feeding of the five thousand, and the four thousand. Jesus prayed a prayer of blessing over the food provided. However, the food multiplied in the disciples' hands. The leader, if in fact that leader is a true servant, is concerned with seeing everyone around them excel. A statement that I have made about my children in particular is that I want each of them to achieve more that I ever dreamed of achieving. Additionally, other people's gifts should never present a threat, or any level of competition, to a leader who is secure within him or herself. There ought to be an environment of safety and security established by the leader that becomes empowering, especially when others are trusted with responsibility that is beyond the menial task. *"After these things the Lord appointed seventy others also, and sent them two by two before His face into every city where He Himself was about to go. Then He said to them: The harvest truly is great, but the laborers are few; therefore pray the Lord of the harvest to send out laborers into His harvest………And heal the sick there, and say to them, the Kingdom of God has come near to you." (Lk 10: 1-2, 9).*

Any great leader is able to recognize greatness, and assist in extracting that greatness, to be served to the masses. Of course, Jesus did operate with a bit of an advantage, since He enjoyed the privilege of foreknowledge. He was empowered with the wisdom of the Ages, which helped greatly in tempering His decisions and movements. Jesus was fully acquainted with the fact that He would be leaving the Earth. He was also aware that the responsibility for advancing the Kingdom was to be left to those He was training. The momentous events of the Book of Acts demonstrates only too well that the students learned very well, as the Kingdom began to grow exponentially. The apostles, as they later became known, were tenacious and aggressive in their task of finishing the work that Jesus had started. It would behove us all as modern day believers to take a page from the apostles' book of servitude, and put aside all of our aspirations for notoriety and acclaim to serve all of humanity.

There are times when I am deeply saddened by the glaring ineptitude in the approach of the modern day church to ministry. We are so fixated on what we are doing in a building that we all but forget about what we should be doing to reach the *fallen* and the *lost*. We enjoy celebrating ourselves while the communities and neighborhoods we have been sent to serve lie around us as wasteland. I would even venture to say that the American church exudes a spirit of arrogance that I have not experienced in many of the nations of the world to

CHAPTER TEN: Jesus Was A Servant Leader

which I have been privileged to travel. The imagery that I often have in my mind is Jesus with a towel wrapped around His waist. He admonished the disciples that they should do for one another what He had done for them. *"So when He had washed their feet, taken His garments, and sat down again, He said to them; Do you know what I have done to you? You call Me Teacher and Lord, and you say well, for so I am. If I then, your Lord and Teacher, have washed your feet, you also ought to wash one another's feet. For I have given you an example, that you should do as I have done to you." (Jn 13: 12-15).* In this day and age, many leaders will have to be identified by their title, or perish the very thought of them condescending to respond to your greeting. However, the example of Jesus demonstrates to us that He was never called Prophet Jesus, or Apostle Jesus, or Reverend Jesus, or Dr Jesus, or Bishop Jesus. Our Lord was simply referred to as Jesus. I often wonder where and when that trend began. In actuality, it was present during the Biblical era as well, and all we in the present age have done is to personify it. *"For it has been declared to me concerning you, by those of Chloe's household that there are contentions among you. Now I say this, that each of you says, I am of Paul, or I am of Apollos, or I am of Cephas, or I am of Christ. Is Christ divided? Was Paul crucified for you? Or were you baptized in the name of Paul?" (1 Cor 1: 11-13).* Of course, these are rhetorical questions with a resounding *"no"* as their answer. The man or woman that sees themselves as some sort of supreme leader places themselves in a very dangerous place. Almighty God has made it quite clear that He will not share His glory with anyone. One of the hallmarks of being a servant leader is to remain constantly approachable. We have seen leaders who have an entourage that will not allow others to come near them, including children. Evidently they don't remember that it was the people who helped put them where they are. This is where Jesus finds Himself in a class all by Himself. *"Then they brought little children to Him, that He might touch them; but the disciples rebuked those who brought them. But when Jesus saw it, He was greatly displeased and said to them; Let the little children come to Me, and do not forbid them; for of such is the Kingdom of God. Assuredly, I say to you, whoever does not receive the Kingdom of God as a little child will by no means enter it!" (Mk 10: 13-15).*

Therefore, the essence of servant leadership is to serve with humility. Jesus performed thousands of miracles, and no matter how remarkable any of them might have been, He never sought accolades or awards for anything that He did. *"For thus says the High and Lofty One who inhabits eternity; whose name is Holy: I dwell in the high and holy place, with him who has a contrite and humble spirit, to revive the spirit of the humble, and to revive the heart of the contrite ones." (Isa 57: 15).* The Hebrew word for contrite is *"Dakka,"* which means to be crushed like powder. Thus, the "wetness" of the Holy Spirit can shape and mold us into what He sees us to be. The sentiment is perfectly understandable that some people feel others will take advantage of them when they constantly maintain a humble spirit. Yet, being meek does not mean that one is weak. Meekness is nothing more than God's power under control. *"Therefore humble yourselves under the mighty hand of God, that He may exalt you in due time." (1 Pet 5:6).*

The Lord is not looking for celebrities in His Kingdom. He is looking for men and women that will follow the example of Jesus, and make impact on Earth through a unique blend of humility and confidence. Eventually the Lord will place us in a position of influence. *"And being found in appearance as a man, He humbled Himself and became obedient to the point of death, even the death of the cross. Therefore God has highly exalted Him and given Him the name which is above every name, that at the name of Jesus every knee should bow, of those in heaven, and of those on earth, and of those under the earth." (Phil 2: 8-10).* The life of a leader is nothing more than emptying oneself so that the Lord can fill one up.

Prayer of Focus

"Lord, help me to discern the meaning of my call to servant leadership, such that I might follow the example of your son, Jesus Christ, our Lord and Savior, who showed us all the greatness of true humility. Fill me with Your grace such that, inspired by the knowledge of Your abiding presence, I can serve others in humility, and be an emitter of Your love and compassion. Finally, teach me to decrease such that others might increase, and to lead with the vision of a faithful follower of Jesus, your Son. In Jesus Name. Amen.

CHAPTER ELEVEN
Jesus Was A Resilient Leader

"O My Father, if it is possible, let this cup pass from Me; nevertheless, not as I will, but as You will." (Mt 26:39)

Resilience is a critical requirement in leadership. Navigating the perilous times, with their inherent challenges, setbacks, disappointments, and uncertainties, is an inevitable part of the leadership journey. Those that work alongside the leader are, as might be expected, on the look out for the intestinal fortitude that should be exhibited by the leader, such they too can develop the stamina that will see them through the challenging times of their own season of leadership. A resilient leader does not wilt under pressure and can even give the impression that what was just experienced was really nothing to fret about. Resilience is a learned behavior that comes with time, after having endured many trials and tribulations. A stoic mindset is cultivated that declares, *"I have reached that place of breakthrough survival because the challenge I am facing is no longer overly impressive!"* Fear, if not conquered, can become a serious impediment to growth. *"There is no fear in love; but perfect love casts out fear, because fear involves torment. But he who fears has not been made perfect in love." (1 Jn 4: 18)*. That sort of mindset can only deter progress and momentum in an organization, since the activities of followers will simply pause as soon as their leader appears to be overwhelmed by the challenges of that leadership role.

But who is a resilient leader? A resilient leader swiftly adapts to change, and seamlessly capitalizes on opportunities. Such a leader recovers from setbacks rather quickly, unearths creative solutions, and inspires others to have a vision for their work and organization. Of greater significance, the resilient leader appears to possess a seamless, fluid response to potential challenges, while positioning the team for the next steps. Without resilient leaders to guide their teams into new arenas of hope and possibilities, organizations will, almost invariably, find themselves stuck when faced with adversity. When an organization is lacking this type of leadership, there are consequences such as, missed opportunities for growth and efficiency, limited innovation, productivity and creativity, and a coterie of unmotivated employees. organizational experiences during the COVID-19 pandemic provide us eloquent examples. COVID-19 brought many challenges to the traditional workplace environment, but organizations with resilient leaders adapted and provided a vision of what could be, and the platform for achieving it. Rather than just see challenges, they also saw opportunities, and this type of leadership is critical. For example, because of the lockdowns decreed by governments all over the world, the first organizational and corporate challenge was how to hold the traditional, yet vital team meetings at which crucial workplace decisions were taken. That was no longer possible with virtually everyone now working from home. Soon enough, leadership resilience and creativity took over. The now ubiquitous zoom video conferencing platform was born, which allows users to create and join virtual meeting rooms where they can communicate with each other using video, and audio. Additional features give participants the ability to share their screen, share files, and use text chat within the meeting group or privately with others in the meeting. That is resilience at play.

When facing a problem, leaders can easily allow a situation to control them, instead of taking control of the situation. Resilient leadership requires leaders to act in an urgent and honest fashion, recognizing that mistakes are inevitable and correcting course without necessarily assigning blame. The resilient leader is *flexible*. A leader needs to be able to bounce back quickly and protect their team. A car bumper is in place to provide bounce back in the event of a collision and protect the passengers. A resilient leader is like the car bumper of the team. They can handle bad news or disgruntled opinions, and can listen and respond constructively. Flexibility alludes to a certain openness to change, adapting to situations, and having the ability to see refreshingly different perspectives and possibilities. The resilient leader is simultaneously *realistic* and *optimistic*. That means they can recognize the problem and look beyond the current situation to paint a positive future on the other side of the canvas of a challenging situation. There is invaluable utility in acknowledging a problem, or a bad situation, and the feelings associated with those unfortunate circumstances, but the key is not becoming overwhelmed by the negativity and pessimism. Resilient leadership focus quickly switches to the solutions.

The resilient leader is *agile*, pivoting and changing direction quickly as the need arises. When leaders are open to suggestions and willing to change how they do things, they will be agile in challenging circumstances. In today's world, in particular, we live and work in uncertain and volatile environments, but resilient leaders can change focus to meet needs, and continue to foster high-performing teams. Most importantly, the resilient leader is emotionally intelligent. Emotional intelligence is the ability to manage and understand your own emotions, and the emotions of those around you. A high index of emotional intelligence allows one to appropriately label feelings and identify how they can affect a situation and other people. The ability to express and control emotions is important, but a resilient leader also needs to be able to interpret and respond to others' emotions and needs. Ultimately, the resilient leader has a *locus of control,* which implies the belief that one has some control over outcomes, situations, or experiences. This sort of control in a resilient leader suggests that the focus is on what can be controlled, rather than what cannot be controlled. Breaking situations down into controllable and uncontrollable categories makes challenges seem smaller and more manageable. Jesus was the quintessential resilient leader.

From the onset of His ministry, there was never a time when He did not exercise His locus of control. There was never a time when He was not in full control of His faculties. There were instances when massive crowds sought His demise, yet He never caved to the taunting and demented howls that tormented Him. Resilient leaders understand and regulate their emotions to avoid stressful panic. Even in moments that could have caused imminent death, He fell into blissful sleep. He even questioned the disciples as to why they disturbed His sleep in the midst of a raging storm. It would seem that if, in fact, the Lord could fall sleep in the midst of hair-raising turbulence, there was absolutely nothing to fear. This indicates that a resilient leader possesses the ability to adapt to evolving circumstances, and to provide stable leadership when others are questioning the outcome. Throughout scripture, not once are we entertained with an instance in which Jesus was not resolute in His decision making and strategizing. *"Then Jesus lifted up His eyes, and seeing a great multitude coming toward Him, He said to Philip; Where shall we buy bread, that these may eat? But this He said to test him, for He Himself knew what He would do!"* (Jn 6: 5-6). This is because resilient leaders

CHAPTER ELEVEN: Jesus Was A Resilient Leader

operate proactively, anticipating challenges and developing inspiring plans to address any and all uncertainty. There is no doubt that the Lord Jesus lived life on a higher plane. The same dimension is available to each one of us that elects to *believe.*

As I have stated in a previous chapter, Jesus came, not only to die for us and as us, but to model and demonstrate exactly who we were supposed to be had Adam and Eve not disobeyed God. On numerous occasions, He challenged the disciples to expand the parameters of their thinking. However, they always had great difficulty in shifting from thinking as *fishermen* to thinking as *Kingdom citizens.* A resilient leader also recognizes the fact that not everyone will grasp what might even be fundamental principles, and remain in patience to learn and grow. Imagine if Jesus had fired Peter? The world would have lost one of the greatest leaders to have been born. Another compelling factor in resilient leadership is the ability to effectively communicate, with transparency being a key element. The Lord never hid the fact that He was going to die a most horrible death, and subsequently leave them.Of course, despite His awareness that the apostles were dismayed at hearing such patently distressing news, He nonetheless kept them informed at all times. The destruction of many ministries and organizations is predicted on the lack of transparent and empathetic communication, especially during traumatic times. To be a resilient leader, it is imperative to be fully aware of your strengths and weaknesses. That awareness provides an indication of what one's responses will be to various forms of adversity, since it allows one to properly assess one's capabilities and limitations. Additionally, it is important that one set some form of standard that will be the leader's guide for life. That way, during tumultuous times, there will be no wavering. The Bible is clear on the fact that a double-minded man is unstable in all of his ways. *"For let not that man suppose that he will receive anything from the Lord; he is a double-minded man, unstable in all his ways." (James 1:7-8).*

Culturally, Jesus lived in a very volatile environment, especially given the fact that even His birth raised perplexities that rendered it questionable, and that is added to the fact that He was raised in a blended family. The people were well aware of that fact, and had no qualms about calling His entire family circumstances into question. Yet another layer to the seemingly unwholesome scenario was the fact that even His own family did not believe in Him. Through their own admission, they stated that they felt He had lost His mind. This was all because He didn't stop to eat lunch during a time of ministering to others. If He hadn't been such a resilient leader, it would have been both easy and reasonable for Him to capitulate to the whims and caprices of His family. Aside from all of what He endured, He needed resilience to handle betrayal and rejection from within His own close circle. Imagine being betrayed by a man who had lived with you for three years, and who then unconscionably secured your death for *just* thirty pieces of silver. Yet, He withstood that terrible betrayal, and then went on to die an excruciating and humiliating death on the cross. Except a man possess incomparable inner strength and extraordinary resolve, there is no way He would survive such agony of the greatest magnitude any human being could conceivably face.

The test of resilience is demonstrated when someone can surrender to a higher purpose at humongous personal cost. The Lord Jesus was fully acquainted with what it would cost Him in the Garden of Gethsemane. During a time of agonizing prayer, He was able to look into the crucible that was His to drink and request that *"If it be possible, let this cup pass from Me."* However, He now employed a word that I personally subscribe to, to totally redirect the narrative. *Nevertheless!*

CHAPTER ELEVEN: Jesus Was A Resilient Leader

"Nevertheless, not My will but Yours be done!" That sort of response can only be summoned from the very core, and the subterranean depths of a person'e being. This is the sort of moment when a resilient leader intentionally chooses *purpose* over *pain*. Such resilience transcends a person beyond mere survival to the perfect willingness to fulfill some purpose that is of far greater magnitude than one's own self-serving preservation. Adversity is an inevitability in our life journey, yet what matters most is how we face it. At any time, Jesus could have summoned legions of angels to assist Him, but He chose to drink the bitter cup presented to Him with dignity, and with grace.

One is drawn to wonder how anyone could possibly withstand the type of punishment Jesus endured without complaining. *"He was oppressed and He was afflicted, yet He opened not His mouth; He was led as a lamb to the slaughter, and as a sheep before its shearers is silent, so He opened not His mouth." (Isa 53: 7-8).* Leaders often discover that true resilience is not merely a *characteristic*, but a *transformative force* capable of converting suffering into triumph, and despair into hope. I am always utterly amazed at how the Lord Jesus stood in the face of massive challenges, undaunted and unafraid. Nothing seemed to faze Him, even after an angry mob attempted to kill Him prematurely. Yet, even after that attempt, He came back to the same place as the altercation the very next day, and once again ministered the gospel of the Kingdom. One can only imagine what our culture and society would look like today if the Body of Christ had that type of resilience. In most instances, our greatest noise is made on a Sunday morning at eleven o'clock, only to be hushed until the clock strikes the same hour on the following Sunday. Indeed, the work is immense, but the laborers are few. I am fully aware of the fact that there have been a few attempts at changing the culture, but the attempts were met with futility. However, we cannot accept failure as a final outcome, but as a stepping stone toward future success. Resilient leaders embrace challenge and change as a catalyst for advancement, and to steer their teams toward strategic foresight. From generation to generation, apostasy seems to grow, even as the world's people become more and more cynical in their thoughts about God. I often wonder why millions of people display such utter disdain at the mention of His name. Yet, the annals of scripture reveal to us that even during the Biblical era, the sentiment was very much the same. Nonetheless, Jesus remained resolute in His desire to see humanity come back to their Creator, and experience His undying and unwavering love for them.

Fast forward to the modern day, and we observe a society and culture that literally thumbs their nose at God. Sadly, the church is complicit in this attitude. Our lukewarm spirit does little to sway the mindset of humankind, since they are unable to observe the fervor and fire that was once the climate of the church; God's own people. It is stated in scripture that we are to first desire to be like Jesus, and then demonstrate His example on Earth, without hesitance or fear. It is quite apparent that we have lost any desire to be confrontational. To put it succinctly, there are very few of us that have the boldness and courage to confront the ills of society head on, and not back down when threatened with reprisals. Again, if we are going to follow the resilient leadership style of Jesus, there can be no room for cowardice. This is a principle that was also taught in the Old Testament. One of the pre-requisites of going to battle was to address and answer the question as to whether or not a man actually wanted to go to war in the first place. *"Now therefore, proclaim in the hearing of the people, saying, 'Whoever is fearful and afraid, let him turn and depart at once from Mount Gilead.' And twenty-two thousand of the people returned, and ten thousand remained." (Judges 7:3).* That was quite startling for the commander of an army; that with one question, you lose two-thirds of your army.

CHAPTER ELEVEN: Jesus Was A Resilient Leader

However, even before Gideon's time, the children of Israel faced other battles where the same question was raised, and more so because fear could very possibly dictate the tenor of the battle. *"The officers shall speak further to the people and say; What man is there who is fearful and fainthearted? Let him go and return to his house, lest the heart of his brethren faint like his heart." (Deut 20:8).*

I would venture to say that such a question is not raised in any congregation today. Our concern is more about church membership than about Kingdom advancement. Jesus was very clear, prior to His departure, *"Occupy until I come!"* These words appeared in a parable. *"And he called his ten servants, and delivered them ten pounds, and said unto them, Occupy till I come." (Lk 19:13).* The translation of the passage actually means to *"Take Care of Business."* Prior to Joshua's death, the Lord confronted him, and said there was still much land to conquer, meaning although the work Joshua did while he was alive was admirable, there was still much land that had not been conquered. A very sad commentary will be written about this generation of believers as there is stillmuch land to conquer. Indeed, I indict today's believer. There are times when I think that the modern day believer is actually what I call an *"unbelieving believer."* Most of us do not consider it even remotely necessary to defend the faith. The Bible says in 1 Pet 3:15, *"But sanctify the Lord God in your hearts, and always be ready to give a defense to everyone who asks you a reason for the hope that is in you, with meekness and fear."* In this passage, Peter is decidedly not speaking of *"trembling in your boots"* kind of fear! His reference is to having a reverential awe for God Almighty. In examining the life of a man like Nelson Mandela, we observe that he was a man of strong conviction, willing to risk his life for what he believed in. He was a man who was not intimidated by the regime of the day, and put his life on the line, only to see him ultimately become president of his country. However, none of this would ever have come to pass had he allowed himself to capitulate to the threats of people who thought that his influence would be hushed by the rocks he was given to break every day while incarcerated. In reality, he broke the rocks, the rocks decidedly did not break him. Additionally, through all he had to endure, he did not allow it to harden him, or corrode his heart. He was able to infinitely forgive, reconcile, and then lead South Africa through a tumultuous experience that totally embodied the transformative power of resilient leadership. Much is to be learned from the type of leadership that refuses to take *"no"* for an answer. To such leadership, failure is unacceptable. That is the sort of man or woman that believes that anything is possible when God is the catalyst that keeps everything together. Dr Myles Munroe had a slogan for his organization, *"The Third World Leaders Association."* It was the place where followers were becoming leaders, and leaders were becoming agents of change.

Jesus carried twelve men with Him for three and a half years, and for the most part, they were being intensely trained to be His replacement because He knew the time of His departure. Even though they stumbled and fumbled their way through the course, once He departed, these men were then referred to by some as the men who turned the world upside down. Jesus, being the ultimate leader, also demonstrated trust in those who followed Him by sending them into places where He would ultimately visit. Trust is the bedrock of effective leadership. People will never realize their full potential by working with a leader who micromanages everything. *"After these things the Lord appointed seventy others also, and sent them two by two before His face and into every city and place He Himself was about to go. Then He said to them; the harvest truly is great, but the laborers are few; therefore pray the Lord of the harvest to send out laborers into His harvest. Go your way; behold, I send you out as lambs among wolves." (Lk 10: 1-3).* That statement, in and of itself, gives rise to the fact that what these men were experiencing was *on-the-job* training. Jesus had to trust that they were going to do the right thing until He arrived. A resilient leader realizes that they must create an environment where others are valued, and ultimately become motivated because of it. The American church has set up a destructive model whereby we have a one-person structure. For the most part, everything revolves around the senior pastor, because of which the other ministry gifts designated in Eph 4 are not even acknowledged. As powerful as Jesus was, He still recognized the need for help. The landscape of society is continuing to change and except we change with it. we are resigning ourselves to a world of darkness. I read a post on Facebook recently. I don't know who the author was, but it said, *"Weare drowning in information, while starving for wisdom! We pride ourselves in all of our technological advances, yet there is really no advancement in our ability to genuinely coexist with one another."* In my opinion, no statement could possibly speak more directly into ineffective leadership.

As I have already stated, I do realize that leadership in the 21st century comes with pressures that were most likely never faced in previous generations. However, I also believe that the one thing that remains constant is human behavior. There are definitely going to be certain nuances that are different only because of the fact of evolution in our creative abilities. Pandemics, climate change, as well as unprecedented global tragedies, call for leaders that have a strong inner resolve to face those conditions head on. Also, corporate America, as well as the church, now have to exist in unaccustomed, hybrid forms in order to meet the demands of modern day life. In the face of this type of novelties, a resilient leader must be flexible, and have a strong set of personal values, and the ability to turn problems into opportunities. This is the continuous and consistent example that Jesus set before His disciples, and which He has left on record for us to follow. What is critically important is that we must always make the *main thing the main thing*. Resilient leaders remained focused on the goal and objective no matter what has happens. *"Looking unto Jesus, the author and finisher of our faith, who for the joy that was set before Him endured the cross, despising the shame, and has sat down at the right hand of the throne of God." (Heb 12: 2).*

Prayer of Focus

Lord, give me strength, and the abiding resilience of spirit, so that I do not grow weary in my leadership role. Father, my task as a leader may seem exhausting and overwhelming, but I pray that I will continue to recognize that the task was assigned to me to do Your will. I pray for divine strength not to rely on me, but on You. In Jesus Name. Amen.

CHAPTER TWELVE

Jesus Was A Creative Communicator

"If the Martin Luther Kings of our world rode the waves of our consciousness as master orators then, through his parables alone, Jesus Christ of Nazareth bequeathed incomparable wisdom and knowledge to the world as Lord of Oratory." Author

From one generation to another, there are many men who have been considered to be some of the greatest orators of their time. These are men who possess the unique ability to weave words together with the incomparable skill and dexterity that leaves others, not only in awe of them, but also clinging to their every word, very much as a baby chick waits to be fed by the mother hen. Undoubtedly, *oratory*, otherwise known as the *gift of the garb,* is a gift that, in our modern day age, is being utilized in ways that are as versatile and profound as *story telling,* and which many have successfully monetized as their vocation. Yet, oratory itself, in the annals of mankind, has its own fascinating history. Oratory was considered an enviable skill in Ancient Rome, a civilization that was incomparably famed for its coterie of philosophers. In fact, Ancient Rome's greatest gift to the world is its philosophers, and none of these revered intellectuals personified the gift of oratory as much as a man named *Cicero*.

Marcus Tullius Cicero lived from January 106 BCto 7 December 43BC. He was a Roman statesman, lawyer, scholar, philosopher, writer and academic sceptic whose extensive writings include treatises on rhetoric, philosophy and politics. He is considered one of Rome's greatest orators and prose stylists, and the innovator of what became known as *Ciceronian rhetoric*. His influence on the Latin language was so immense that he wrote fully three-quarters of the Latin literature that is known to have existed in his lifetime. Easily considered one of the most prolific Roman writers, the number of his speeches, letters and treatises that have survived into the modern era is a testament to his admiration by successive generations. These days, it is not uncommon to see acknowledged orators referred to as *Cicero of our times*, and the world has simply not been in short supply of such iconic individuals.

As we gaze back into history, for instance, we cannot but recall men such as Abraham Lincoln, whose speech, *The Gettysburg Address,* has etched itself eternally in the minds of many as a piece of oratory that is a cornerstone of the annals of the American epoch. There is no doubt that people are drawn to individuals who possess uncommon linguistic skills, and will readily follow such people, if only because, in being adept at passionately expressing the views they espouse, they are in the same instance capable of convincing their audience of the combined veracity and credibility of those views. President John F. Kennedy was one such leader. He managed to leave an indelible oratorical imprint on the world with the speech he gave in front of the Berlin Wall. In managing to convince them that they would not be occupied by East Germany, that speech brought a sense of hope and encouragement to the people of West Germany.

Nelson Mandela was of the same ilk. He joined the African

CHAPTER TWELVE: Jesus Was A Creative Communicator

National Congress in 1944, and was arrested in 1962 for crimes that were alleged to be tantamount to treason. He would spend the next twenty seven years in jail, and time after time, he spoke out from prison in such a way that he would eventually be granted his freedom, to ultimately become the president of post-apartheid South Africa. Passion is a key element in exceptional communication. Amelia Earhart was a repository of such passion. Sometimes, it can be a tool of great utility to employ contrast to associate the *unfamiliar* with the *familiar*. Being a woman in her era, she became a spokesperson for many women who aspired to be aviators. Dr Martin Luther King Jr's speech, *I Have A Dream,* remains a classic to this day, and continues to have a spellbinding effect on its listeners.

Yet, even with all of these aforementioned *Ciceros*, none comes remotely close to the oratorical genius of Jesus. He was undoubtedly a master storyteller who always seemed to know what to say at any given time to capture the minds and attention of whomever He was communicating with. Whether He was speaking with someone who was destitute, or a high ranking government or spiritual leader, He knew exactly how to engage each person as to effectively convey His message. Parables, in many instances, were His favorite oratorical tools for demystifying seemingly complex subjects. A parable is nothing more than a short allegorical story designed to illustrate or teach some truth, religious principle, or moral lesson. Another perfectly valid definition of a parable is *"An Earthly story with a heavenly meaning,"* and if the Martin Luther Kings of our world rode the waves of our consciousness as master orators then, through his parables alone, Jesus Christ bequeathed incomparable wisdom and knowledge to the world as *Lord of Oratory.* Jesus was parable personified.

Far from necessarily seeking to impress His listeners with His oratorical skills, however, Jesus had specific reasons for teaching in parables. *Why, indeed, did Jesus teach in parables?* Before we answer this question, we need to understand what parables *truly* are. We know that the gospels record 39 distinct parables of Jesus, ranging from the *Parable of the Old Garment,* which is given in only one verse, "Then He spoke a parable to them: *"No one puts a piece from a new garment on an old one; otherwise the new makes a tear, and also the piece that was taken out of the new does not match the old." (Lk 5:36),* to the *Parable of the Prodigal Son,* which is covered in some 21 verses (Lk 15:11–32). Some parables are unique, being found in only one of the gospel narratives, while the other parables appear in each of the gospels. The Gospel of John contains no parables, at least not as parables are commonly understood. This is because John's focus was more on recording Jesus' teaching narratives, especially to his disciples.

The word *parable* in Greek literally means *"to come alongside."* Parables, then, were short stories given by Jesus in order "to come alongside" His listeners, and to teach significant spiritual truths. Since they convey more than just a moral truth, parables are not fables; and since they focus upon more than just words and phrases, parables are not metaphors. Actually, parables must be seen as a unique genre of storytelling that were accorded their place of pride in literature by Jesus, and He used them to fulfill His purpose, especially when speaking to large crowds (Matt 13:34). To the modern reader, at first glance, parables may seem like colorful examples that merely clarify Jesus' teachings. Today's Christian may even assume that Jesus primarily used parables to explain His doctrines, which may have seemed complex to the common crowds. Yet, this might be an oversimplification of the motive behind Jesus' use of parables.

So, why did Jesus conduct His oratory in parables? I invite you to observe that after giving the Parable of the Soils,

CHAPTER TWELVE: Jesus Was A Creative Communicator

which is recorded in all three of the gospels of Matthew, Mark and Luke, and before He explained its meaning, Jesus was asked by His disciples, *"Why do You speak to the crowds in parables?" (Matt. 13:10).* No one can say the precise reason why the apostles asked this question. Perhaps the disciples were afraid that the people did not quite understand Jesus' teachings. Regardless of the rationale for the disciples' question, Jesus' answer about His use of parables is both *surprising* and *instructive.* Jesus replied that He taught in parables for this reason, *"Because it has been given to you to know the mysteries of the kingdom of heaven, but to them it has not been given." (Matt 13:11).* To express it differently, *the reason why Jesus taught in parables was not to explain spiritual truths to the crowds, but to keep spiritual truths from the crowds.* Lest we doubt or misunderstand His answer, Jesus noted that the veiling of spiritual truths from the unbelieving crowds is actually a fulfillment of Old Testament prophecy given in Isa. 6:9-10. *"And He said, "Go, and tell this people: 'Keep on hearing, but do not understand; Keep on seeing, but do not perceive.' "Make the heart of this people dull, And their ears heavy, And shut their eyes; Lest they see with their eyes, And hear with their ears, And understand with their heart, And return and be healed."* On his own part, Luke said in his narrative, *"And Jesus said to the disciples, 'To you it has been given to know the mysteries of the kingdom of God, but to the rest it is given in parables, so that, "Seeing they may not see, and hearing they may not understand"' (Luke 8:10).*

Now, we are faced with a dilemma. *Why would Jesus purposefully veil the truth from unbelievers?* Our easiest way out is to note that the condition of the unbelieving crowds was both a *natural* result of their own rejection of Christ's message, and a *divine* response of judicial blinding on account of their sin. *"And for this reason God will send them strong delusion, that they should believe the lie, that they all may be condemned who did not believe the truth but had pleasure in unrighteousness." (2 Thess 2:11-12).* Indeed, whenever spiritual truth is communicated, be it plainly or in parables, acceptance will always result in understanding and growth, while rejecting truth will always result in confusion and hardness of the heart. Yet, we must be consoled by the fact that, as we read Jesus' parables, we can be confident that while certain of the parables may be very challenging to understand, the Holy Spirit who dwells in us will *"......... guide you into all truth; for He will not speak on His own authority, but whatever He hears He will speak; and He will tell you things to come." (John 16:13),* and God's Word, which contains parables, is truth. Ultimately, we must always evaluate ourselves, and others, in light of God's Word in order to make sure that our lack of understanding of a given parable is not a symptom of a wider rejection of spiritual truth.

As we journey through the New Testament, we can only be in awe of how Jesus was able to command the attention of large crowds that would follow Him for days at a time; hungering not just for the natural food He provided, but also the spiritual banquet that was served each time he opened His mouth. *"So there was a division among the people because of Him. Now some of them wanted to take Him, but no one laid hands on Him. Then the officers came to the chief priests and Pharisees, who said to them, "Why have you not brought Him?" The officers answered, "No man ever spoke like this Man!" (Jn 7:43-46).* Present day leaders would do themselves a world of favor by studying the communication skills Jesus demonstrated. He always made each story relatively easy to understand. Yet, there were times when He spoke to certain groups of people with the intent of challenging their way of thinking. *"And Jesus said: For judgement I have come into this world, that those who do not see may see, and that those who see may*

CHAPTER TWELVE: Jesus Was A Creative Communicator

be made blind. Then some of the Pharisees who were with Him heard these words and said to Him; Are we blind also? Jesus said to them; If you were blind, you would have no sin, but now you say, we see; therefore your sin remains." (Jn 9: 39-41). This statement ties in perfectly with my previous submission on the purpose of Jesus' parables, because to the average hearer, what He articulated was quite perplexing, even somewhat a paradox. However, to the spiritual mind, it is obvious that He is attempting to raise their dimension of spiritual consciousness. Jesus was attempting to get them to understand that the "blindness" to which He so cryptically referred was to be separated from anything that would create separation between the individual and God. The Pharisees felt that they could "see" because they were the religious order of the day. Yet, in their supposed "sight," they were actually blind to what the Master was trying to teach them. As I have also stated previously, Jesus had the benefit of foreknowledge and discernment, therefore He knew who would understand and who wouldn't.

Some of us might be inclined to wonder why Jesus would elect to *"go round in circles,"* so to speak, if bringing sinners to repentance was His purpose. Yet, it remains quite evident that the Pharisees and Sadducees were intent on being rid of Jesus and His influence. In a manner of speaking, Jesus was clearly *bad* news for their business. After all, as the people were following Him and receiving His teaching, they were not going to the synagogue, and that translated to loss of vital revenue for the high priest. This leads seamlessly to the point that any excellent communicator is able to wield tremendous influence amongst others. In leadership, people are looking for the individual who is able to convincingly articulate truths that they can both identify with, and support. That was why, at times, tens of thousands followed Jesus and even supported Him financially. When telling stories, Jesus had a knack for helping those He spoke *to* see themselves in the people He spoke *of.* We see a perfect example of this in Luke 15, in the story of the prodigal son. The youngest son of an affluent family is totally representative of worldly life; selfish, and without direction and purpose. The father is a loving and compassionate man who had only the best intentions for his two sons. The eldest son exhibits the demeanor of a person who wished to try some of the things his younger brother ventured out to do, but didn't have the courage to do so. It has to make one wonder how he knew so much of what his absentee brother was doing. At the core of the story, however, God's grace is made manifest, and that His love is not withdrawn because a person makes unwise choices and unsound decisions. Ultimately, the parable of the prodigal son teaches us many important lessons, including the importance of *repentance, forgiveness,* and *redemption.* In summary, the story of the Prodigal Son begins with a young man who leaves his father's house to pursue a life of sin. He squanders his father's money on wine, women, and gambling. Eventually, he finds himself in a foreign country, penniless and alone. He decides to return home to his father, hoping to be forgiven and taken back in. When he returns, his father is overjoyed to see him. He immediately forgives his son and welcomes him back with open arms. This story teaches us the importance of repentance and forgiveness. It also shows us the power of redemption.

Prayer of Focus

Lord, give me grace to communicate like Christ Jesus. Allow me to understand my audience, and to know what they need to hear. Holy Spirit, be theorchestrator of my words. Allow me to speak from God's righteousness, such that my message will not necessarily be wise and persuasive words, but words that will demonstrate Your power. Give me faith that will not rest on human wisdom, but faith that will encourage others in the application of their own faith. Holy Spirit, guide my words so that they will be meaningful and believable. Grant

CHAPTER TWELVE: Jesus Was A Creative Communicator

me discernment in both speech and hearing. In Jesus Name. Amen.

EPILOGUE

A World In Need of Authentic Leadership

"And whoever desires to be first among you, let him be your slave; just as the Son of Man did not come to be served, but to serve, and to give His life a ransom for many." (Matt 20:27-28)

If you are reading these words, it only means you have taken the trouble to journey with me through the pages of this book. I thank you for that. Accept my sincere gratitude for making my effort a worthwhile one. Any road, in this journey of life, can be long, hard and arduous. It is harder still if there is no hand to hold as you trudge along, weary from the burden of it all. The effort of writing this book itself was a journey all by itself. In reading this book to the end, you were merely accompanying me on the journey. Thank you for holding my hand, even as I held your own hand, as we made the journey together to discover, and to espouse on, the leadership strategies of our Lord, Jesus Christ.

Christian leadership is peculiar. That is because those who are fundamentally expected to take Jesus' model of leadership to heart; leaders in the Body of Christ, do not have the *martial* authority of military leaders, nor do they have the *financial* muscles of the corporate titans. They only have leadership skills on which to rely. That is why I have taken the monumental trouble of delving so deeply into the leadership style of Jesus Christ. It is those leadership skills that will define whether Christian leaders will truly succeed in their mission of shepherding the flock. Ultimately, what this book aims to accomplish is to highlight the inescapable fact that the only place where Christian leaders will find the leadership principles needed to lead is in God's Word.

Having come this far, I believe we can define Christian leadership as the act of influencing and serving others, based on Christ's will for their lives, so that they can accomplish God's purposes for and through them. Therefore, Christian leadership is not rooted in worldly notions of success, such as the love of money or power. Jesus Himself was clear on this point. *"But Jesus called them to Himself and said, "You know that the rulers of the Gentiles lord it over them, and those who are great exercise authority over them. Yet it shall not be so among you; but whoever desires to become great among you, let him be your servant. And whoever desires to be first among you, let him be your slave; just as the Son of Man did not come to be served, but to serve, and to give His life a ransom for many." (Matt 20:25-28).* In other words, leaders are not to oppress and overpower others with their authority, like the Gentiles did. Instead, leaders are supposed to serve others, which Jesus Himself demonstrated when He *"made Himself of no reputation, taking the form of a bondservant, and coming in the likeness of men. And being found in appearance as a man, He humbled Himself and became obedient to the point of death, even the death of the cross" (Phillipians 2:7-8).*

I will wrap up this book by declaring that, when all is said and done, Jesus exemplified the Christian leadership principles of *love, modesty, humility, integrity,* and *total submission to the will of the Father.* Sadly, our modern day culture leaves us longing for, and languishing in need of, leadership that might, in even some small way, resemble the remarkable and exemplary model of Jesus. In the tapestry of leadership, Jesus' style stands out as a timeless masterpiece, woven together with cords, not only of *love, modesty, humility, integrity,* and *submission,* but also *of compassion, vision, inclusion,* and *resilience.* As leaders struggle with the nuances of the 21st century, the leadership style of Jesus serves as a source of inspiration, and a sign post for navigating the intricacies of the overall human experience.

There can be no doubt that in focusing on His leadership abilities, we find a rather profound and all-inclusive philosophy that extends beyond the boundaries of time and culture, and which ought to be attractive to leaders who aspire to lead with purpose, compassion and long lasting impact. It is also clear that His focus was on the *struggles* and *hardships* of a fallen humanity, and that He dedicated Himself to patching the gaping holes that existed in the fabric of the lives of the majority of the people He encountered. It is refreshing to visualize a leader who believed that no one was beneath His touch. In sharp contrast, our modern age of globalization merely continues to set in very stark terms the impersonality in the relationship between *leaders* and the *led.* The average leader is no more that a celebrity that seeks adulation and applause from a fawning followership.

I take my leave from these pages by soberly declaring that our society as a whole will not improve an iota until everyone is seen as a person of *value.* At the same time, even when and where that holds as sacrosanct truth, it will not have great impact until every individual sees him or herself as possessing that *value,* and strongly desires to be a worthy contributor to the overall good of mankind. In the final analysis, the leadership legacy of Jesus beckons leaders to move beyond *transactional* success, and to embrace a *transformative* vision that will leave an indelible mark on individuals, organizations, and the world at large. Thank you, and God bless you for keeping the faith with me.

THE ULTIMATE LEADER

Gilbert Coleman
Philadelphia, Pennsylvania
February 2024

Printed in the USA
CPSIA information can be obtained
at www.ICGtesting.com
LVHW051930240924
791985LV00019B/294